First published in Great Britain in 1997

1 3 5 7 9 10 8 6 4 2

Lyrics reproduced by permission of EMI/Complete

Some text reproduced by kind permission of *Loaded* magazine

The *Screamadelica* 'sun' was created by Paul Cannell

Ebury Press
Random House, 20 Vauxhall Bridge Road, London SW1V 2SA

Random House Australia (Pty) Limited
20 Alfred Street, Milsons Point, Sydney, New South Wales 2061, Australia

Random House New Zealand Limited
18 Poland Road, Glenfield, Auckland 10, New Zealand

Random House South Africa (Pty) Limited
Endulini, 5A Jubliee Road, Parktown 2193, South Africa

Random House UK Limited Registration Number 954009

A CIP catalogue records for this book is available from the British Library

ISBN 0 09 186321 X

Designed at mokom™

Printed and bound in Great Britain by Butler and Tanner Limited, Frome, Somerset

Papers used by Ebury Press are natural, recyclable products made from wood grown in sustainable forests.

Médecins Sans Frontières is the world's largest independent organisation for emergency medical relief. In sixty-four countries world-wide, MSF provides relief to the victims of war and natural disaster irrespective of race, religion or political affiliation.
It doesn't hurt to help.

For more information, contact:
MSF UK 124-132 Clerkenwell Road, London EC1R 5DL
Telephone: 0171 713 5600
Fax: 0171 713 5004
Email: office@london.msf.org

Be responsible for your actions. Act on your responsibilities.

primal scream

higher than than the sun.

grant fleming

Picture by Bobby Gillespie, New York, February, 1994

Grant Fleming

Stepney London E1, 1960. Jumped through my drum kit, my party 1966. Newting 1968. Longest Snog Award, Owen's party 1970. Donkey Derby winner, 1972.

Out all night, police come looking, Faces/New York Dolls, 1972. Bunking-in for Bowie, Romford 1973. Cockney cup final 1975, Anderlecht got our cup, 1976. Threads ripped to shreds 1977. I fought the law and the law definitely won, 1977-1982. Sham army/Jam barmy 1977-1980. A Kid Next Door 1978-80. *Brooking on the head!*

Freedom? There ain't no fucking freedom! June 1980. Up and down a green and (un)pleasant land – Inter-City, of course, 1976-82. Playing with Agent Orange and Tin Soldiers 1982-1985. Spain '82, Mexico '86, Italia '90. 'Need any dusters?' The Knockers 1982 *and* 1993.

ESPANA! 1985. And I think to myself, what a wonderful world.

Hollywood highs with the Lords of the New Church, 1985-87. Tying the knot in New Orleans 1987. On the trail of the contras 1988.

Wapping, the Nurses, the Miners – where were you?

Smile so wide 1989-90. Could it ever get better? Direction. Reaction. Creation 1990-91. Higher Than The Sun 1990-95. Kings for a day – Poll Tax, London 1990. Gulf mooching 1991. Cuba Si, 1992. Cambodia Free, 1993. Nelson we love you – the greatest party there'll ever be, Jo'Burg, 1994.

Chasing the eclipse, South America and India, 1994-5. Getting *loaded* and certainly trying to have a good time, 1994 – ?

Acknowledgements

FOR HELP ON THIS BOOK ...
Jake Lingwood - I don't know if there's anyone else who could have edited this book. Thanks for the belief and encouragement. Mark Bown aka Typo, and Brendan, you did me proud. Maggio di Madark for the twenty-four-hour advice line, you're the daddy. Simon top-scan and Micro on the bike. Dean Marsh the legal eagle. Sandra at Joe's Basement (Wardour St.) for economic assistance and enthusiasm. John Newman the master printer. Mum for help with the hardware. Sister Dany for help with the software. Maggie Noach for trying. Alex and the Scream for the room to swing my cat in. Alan McGee, Tim Abbot, Jeff Barrett and Martin Kelly, for positive support.

And of course the PRIMAL SCREAM TEAM without whom ...

Bob G, Robert the Throb and Andrew Innes - Thanks for the lift and a top night out.
Alex Nightingale, Luce and Tines, neighbours in EC1. Monsieur Dufoir, Denise Johnson, Gentleman H, Toby the big man, Hugo, Steve Sidelnyk, Mani YMG, Paul Mulreany, Murray the muzz, Trigger, Hartie, Fatty, Jason Caulfield, Chilled Chrissie Ridge, the Oz man and Jacko (Manchester vibes in the area), Simon Stevens, Joss, Needsy, Harry Hypno, Mick Shipley, Noel Thompson, Thomas Whitelaw. Tasherini, Simone and Jack. Karen Parker and Christine Wanless. Em Hughes, Anita and Alison. Della and Ray.Dave Joy. Steph, Liz, Lisa, Louise and the very lovely Annie Nightingale. Mr Paul Cannell.

Douglas Hart, Tim Tooher and Angus Cameron. Ed the Ball. Creation Records the 88-90 crew. The Judge and the Archbishop. Masahiro, Mr. Shin and all at Smash. Tomo, Kondi and Kenji. Paul Hutton, Mick Griffiths, the SJM boys, Lees and West, Gerard and Steve down under. Las, Justin and Kev out west. Debs, Sandy, Jane, Tomo, and Sean for keeping me fed with a top bit of tucker. Irvine Welsh, The Sheer Taft, Terry the Chem, Chrissy Abbot, Big Bob and K the H.

There's countless more who've served, I hope you're all still in one piece ...

All the DJs who kept it buzzing, especially Andrew Weatherall, Paul Oakenfold, Alex Paterson, Justin Robertson and Craig Walsh. And, of course, all the residents of the acid house – you made me smile.

THANKS TO THOSE WHO HAVE BEEN THERE ALONG THE WAY ...
Mum, Dad, Brenda, Dany and all my family. Heidi (Moi Kilpe), Ivor Wilkins, Mr Martin Stacey and Jennifer long-socks, Mick and Caroline, Kevin Bridgey, Naughty Norm and Loopy Lou. Andy Swol, Jean Bong, Ian and Kim. Macka of LFC, Jacko of Woolwich (top man). Chris Pope, the Colonel Kevin Peters, Ian the fan Ballinger and Edward J. Halpin. Mary O'Leary, Nancy and her visionary guidance, V.J.P., Debbie Allan, Gina P and Lisa B. John Cracknell, Francesca, Gavino and famiglia Nesi. Steve Rozz for ever, Hilaria, Gaia and the Florentines. Yoli and Mamen. The far gone Doctor John for generosity, support and a bed on several continents. Cat, Sodge, Spike and Pedro and all who kept it coming at Fifth Column. Sue and Andy at Hand Clothing likewise. Nicky Turner, Brian James and Mark Taylor (we had a laugh). Johnny, Vicki and Nick in Perth. Jagzini himself. Jess and Chloe. Rob, Jimmy, John, and all you luvverly girls and boys of the Medicine Bar N1. Lou and Zee Disgracelands. Nina Karenina and Anna Haigh. The Madark posse (Bev, Nicolai, Bailey, Mystic and the Spence). Dierdre O'Callaghan. Peter Jones the Ciba king and Kerry Phillips for telling me I was an asthete when I thought I was a football hooligan. The probation officer who showed me the other route out of Stratford Court. Pedro Rohmanyi, Simon Halfon and BP Fallon. eh Jackie Barron and cool man Wiz the irrepressible one. Ronski, Eric and Tina. Felipe Lettersten; genius, inspiration and unbreakable spirit – the world needs more people like you. Jeff Perks and David Hoffman for encouragement and advice – respect to you both. And your work. Shovello, Roy Pollard and all who helped at the Great Ormond St party. The Greatest London Radio Station. *The* man Don McCullin. Pennie Smith. Bob Matthews, Perry, Dylan and John the Lock. Gerry Lammin, Iestyn George and Alex Griffiths.

Paul Weller for ringing my house with the tour dates as he promised to back in '78. I respect a man who keeps his promise.Eduardo Valderruten and family and every generous soul that's helped me along on my travels around this planet. And there have been far too many to mention. Bless 'em all.

The whole world will be my nation (CeCe Rogers).

James Brown and Tim Southwell for having a look and giving it a go. Thanks fellas. Good work and all that. And all the Loaded crew for getting behind me, and more importantly for having it, wherever the location (Oi! Oi!).

Amanda Baker. Thank-you for putting up with the loco. I don't know how. This book, is in part, down to you. I Love Ya.

Finally, to the three inspirational people who at different times in my life have carved out a path for me. Nan Farfort. James T. Pursey. Alan McGee.
Eternal thanks.

Do not try this at home.

a foreword from primal scream

My brightest star's my inner light, let it guide me
Experience and innocence bleed inside me
Hallucinogens can open me or untie me
I drift in inner space, free of time
I find a higher state of grace, in my mind

I'm beautiful, I wasn't born to follow
I live just for today, don't care about tomorrow
What I've got in my head you can't buy, steal or borrow
I believe in live and let live
I believe you get what you give

I've glimpsed, I have tasted, fantastical places
My soul's an oasis, higher than the sun

I'm higher than the sun

GILLESPIE. INNES. YOUNG.
July 1997

P.S. How are we supposed to remember if he's telling the truth?
– Andrew Innes.

WHEN I GET BAD FEELINGS
I NEED SPIRITUAL HEALING
GOTTA GET ON THE SOUL TRAIN
STOP ME GOING INSANE
I TAKE A GIANT STEP
WITH COLTRANE
JOHN COLTRANE
JOHN COLTRANE
KILL THE PAIN
WITH COLTRANE

prologue

Ronnie Lane is dead. Long live Ronnie the mod. The enigmatic Small Faces/Faces bassist and writer today lost the fight against the bastard MS. It's a sad one. Robert Elms plays 'All or Nothing' and 'Someday' by CeCe Rogers on the radio. I dig out a Faces tape given me by Bob G a couple of years back and whip on 'Ooh La La'. How could you not cry? It's fitting that this is where the story begins.

1972, Wembley Empire Pool. The New York Dolls have just left the building and on bowl the Faces, Rod and the boys. As large as it could get. It's the night of my life so far. I'm twelve years old and knocking about with the big kids, drinking scotch and giving it the big 'un. Nothing had ever excited me quite like this. In a drunken haze later, round the Smith brothers' house, I'm dragged from my slumber at the crack of dawn by a search party comprising the old bill and my mum, who's going off alarming for me staying out, and clips come winging around my ear.

The Faces, twin town Primal Scream, their spiritual sons. Is it any wonder our paths later cross?

Eighteen years later. 1990. By way of Bowie, the Jam, Sham and the Clash. The summer of love just won't end and along comes 'Loaded'. You hear it out, it's the soundtrack to many a claim for 'best night of my life', and the excitement's the same. I walk into Future in London's West End. The Scream come flying by me, bumrushed from the bogs by some bouncers grim (can't always do a line in the ladies).

It can only be a matter of time.

GRANT FLEMING
5 June 1997

1990

Life's drifting a bit. I got a bit carried away in the acid house; me and Heidi split up. Haven't got a bean. Ivor Nesquik gets me selling T-shirts for the House of Love. The nightclubs of Great Britain are on fire. A never-ending tour gets me to see the best of them and that's how I start knocking about with Creation supremo Alan McGee. On his occasional forays up the motorway to check out his charges he'd always be up for it. The HOL were more your post-gig hotel-bar types, lovely geezers that they were (and a fine band to boot), but me and Alan, and whoever else was on it, would be searching for the dawn.

One night/morning we end up in a double-moody party in Chapeltown, Leeds. It's like a dealer's after hours in the back of a terraced house with loads of little firms facing each other off in the barely lit haze of dry ice and puff. Ridiculously though, our amphetamine courage knows no bounds and we bounce around the place on the high of the time. We've got the world's nicest geezer, Ed Ball, for back-up and the Valentines' Anne-Marie, who we have to tone down. Being, it appears, the only woman in the room, her slinky moves on the dancefloor are getting 'em all wild and she's in danger of being leapt on by an ever-encroaching charlie-charged mob. We leave as as some wide-eyed skinheads, who I'd swear were glued up, come charging down the road smacking cars with bats.

Beats a night in with the pipe and slippers.

'I know what you can do. You should manage Primal Scream, Granty.' McGee at this moment is my new best mate and he's trying to find me a job. Fast. He's talking *very* fast, leaping round the room even quicker. 'No, Alan, they're too rock 'n' roll for me, that's over mate, all I care about now is house music all night long. *House music all night long. House music all night long.*' Singing as I finger-dance my way to go try and piss. Nope, no luck again. I'll be back.

I'd had my days of wearing leathers, having played bass mid-eighties with goth-rockers the Lords of the New Church. Soon after we split, came the revolution and 'warrior bass' was no more. Not interested. Pill-popping rather than string-plucking. Rock 'n' roll was dead! I'd been introduced by old ICF hooligan pals to Paul Oakenfold's winning ways, as prior enemies hugged and kissed around me, there was no going back. Everything I'd hoped for at Wapping and with the miners. *We are together.* The kids are united. I hadn't even looked at another band since, save for New Order, and even then Hooky had got me thrown off the stage at Reading for dancing the madman, hood up an' all. No, rock 'n' roll and the house scene just couldn't mix. Huge egos to nil. No competition. Why on earth would I want to get involved with Primal Scream, Alan?

Then along came 'Loaded'.

Alan McGee did find me a job, for which I tip my hat. That's what brings me to this point. Given the offer of running the ever-growing dance division of Creation Records, I bit his hand off. Right up my alleyway. Charging about, day and night, in and out of clubs with a smile on my face. Nothing new there, but being paid for it? Yes, luvverly. This is post-'Loaded' and my thoughts of Primal Scream are different again. Well, that's obvious, how could it not be? Guitars as well. I hold my hands up.

I soon bump into Bobby Gillespie on the back stairs of Creation HQ, sited above a sweatshop in Hackney. (That was a great convenience for bands touting demos: if they didn't get a deal at least they could get their hems done.) It soon becomes obvious that there's a parallel to our lives and our loves, despite growing up in cities 400 miles apart. It's our age. Getting excited in one breath about 'Jail Guitar Doors' (the Clash) and in the next making arrangements for the next Boys' Own.

Ibiza '90. A defining moment. Whilst balearic king Alfredo is finishing his sets at Pacha with 'Loaded', our man Andy Weatherall flies in direct from the mix and strolls into the room promising great things. With an acetate wedged under his arm, he says you'll absolutely love it, just wait and see. Later, at 6 am, the sun lights the dancefloor and the madness of the Ku club. We're flying on saucers …

'Today is a beautiful day!
It is a new day.
We are together!'

Oh-oh, what's going on here?

'Cos together we got power.'

It's Jesse Jackson man. In Ibiza! I swear to God he's in here somewhere.

'Today on this programme you will hear gospel, and rhythm and blues. And jazz.'

And then the highest high-hat you'll ever hear. This is getting silly.

'We know that music is just music.'

Kickdrum! … to heaven … ten minutes up there in the sky…

'Brothers and sisters, the name of the game is power. We are together.'

Never to be forgotten. Welcome to the sound of summer. I lost count of how many times I heard that mix of 'Come Together' in a club. Proper hands-in-the-air gear as well.

I soon feel like the most popular man in the land as Creation becomes a buzz name high on the hiplist. It's no surprise. Driving the country with a bootful of 'Come Together' white labels, and surviving the miles on a pocketful of white. They were ringing me up and begging for 'em – DJs, shops, blaggers. You can't blag a blagger. They were good days, that's for sure. Doors opening all over the show. Strangely enough, it all seemed to go so fast. Pure at the Milk Bar every Wednesday, DJ Danny Rampling at the helm, Clash man Mick Jones rapping in the corner with Innes, and all we did is dance, dance, dance. Monkey Drum Monday, Yellow Book Friday. The weekends wherever, and whatever was happening. Too much to choose from.

It was in the Yellow Book that McGee recalls his favourite Scream tale. He claims Bobby was talking to him and in mid-sentence threw up, all over Alan's threads, and, without missing a beat, Bobby attempted to flick it off, before carrying on the conversation where he left off. I can't vouch for that, but I do remember a particularly tasty dance move Bobby cut that night which saw him fly off the stage and skid 'cross the floor. He was okay, but those white jeans never got over it.

So off to Japan for a Primal Scream tour, unfortunately bang in the middle of the World Cup, Italia '90. I'd sloped off to Sardinia for stage one, but was faced with a terrible dilemma. On to the mainland for stage two or return to London to join the Scream for their first live dates for the 'Loaded' generation? Well, there's a lot worse problems to have, I admit, but as I hadn't been to the Far East before, it got the vote, with a vow to return to Rome forthwith should we reach the final. Besides , I'd just about had enough of some idiots churlishly dragging the cross of St George around. You're on a wonderful sunny isle, full of life, full of colour and where people actually pay to go holiday. Why the long faces? Why the attitude? I admit the police at times were a bit hectic, but lighten up, boys. Enjoy it – you really do only live once. It's obvious the pills hadn't found their way on to those terraces yet …

I hadn't seen Primal Scream live, and, to be honest, knew little of their back catalogue. How were they going to cope with the sound of the dancefloor? Was it possible, or was it going to be white boy rock-out?

For me, there wasn't a band that had achieved that crossover – the Mondays were close enough, but I still thought there was more you could do with it.

Saturday afternoon at the end of June, what a lovely time to fly. Japan Airlines flight 422 to Tokyo. Excitement all round as the sake kicks in. The only members on board who had been East before are Henry the bass and Toby the toms, who'd served under Nico some time before. It's a relatively small contingent – five in the band, Hypnotone's Tony Martin taking care of programming, tour manager Simon Stevens, sound man Noel – who these days is doing the deed with Dodgy – and DJ and spiritual adviser Tim the Tooher. And me. Taking care of merchandising in one hat, representing Creation in another. From what I'd been told the trip would be hell, the band were impossible to be with on the road and were bound to get out of control. Though I expected plenty of rock 'n' roll behaviour, I can't say I was overly worried – I'd been about a bit and whatever way it turned out I was off to Japan on a freemans and there was no way I wasn't going to enjoy that.

In a forerunner to what would later become a ritual on planes, a game of 'pass the temaze' breaks out, and before long there's not a soul left standing. And then you wake up in Japan. On the runway.

All other passengers disembarked. A stewardess shaking your arm. Dribble everywhere. Blimey, whose stag night was that?

Manoeuvring through the arrivals hall is not funny, and if you think that customs will have any sympathy for a hangover, forget it. No, you're going to get a chart full of cartoon narcotics, needles and firearms thrust in your face. I swear he points to every last pill, every last bullet, shouting, 'You have?!!'
'No, Guv.'
Next one. 'You HAVE?!!!!'
'No, mate.'
Next. 'YOU HAVE?!!!!'
'NO-OOOOOO!'
By the time he gets to the pistol I don't half wish I had one.

Now as I'm trying to slip in the country as a tourist, due to not being in possession of a work permit, I keep my distance from the others. Problem is, back at Heathrow I'd stuffed any bags that had room in them full of swag. As bag after bag is opened around me T-shirts and photos tumble out, but, oddly enough, at customs they don't give a damn. Funny that, they were soaked in LSD.

If only. Word is soon out that there's barely a blimp of puff in town, let alone anything else, but for a band with a rep for drug-ravaged madness no one seems arsed. The ride into the city goes on for hours, the roads are rammo, it's overcast and there's not a green space in sight. In fact, there's no space whatsoever. You couldn't slip a Rizla between those buildings. I come from a city, a great big mother of one at that, but I've never seen anything quite like this.

We check into the Creston Hotel – seems like a nice place. Very new. Rooms are a bit small, though.

Despite the travel weariness we're summoned to dinner with local promoters Smash, and joined by writer James Havoc, Brighton associate of the band who'd made his own way. The city is a neon overdose, hard to take in at this point, and even though it's Sunday it's busy, busy, busy. The food is great, though, the beer's not half bad either, which, as I remember, leads members of the band off on a rant about how pish the Soup Dragons are.

By the early hours we're wide awake again, which is just as well as we've got West Germany v. the Czechs first, then a game of high drama in which England scrape through against the amazing Lions of Cameroon. Who will ever forget Roger Milla and the corner-flag dance? This now has me ranting, 'If we beat West Germany I'm going to Rome. No! *When* we beat West Germany I'm going to …' etc., etc. Innes finally feigns tiredness and turfs me out of his room.

With your body-clock all over the place and the searing midsummer heat frying your brain just a walk up the road whacks you full out. And it's humid, man. The sweat falls off you and it's a shower per hour. Me, Bobby and Harry Hypno (Tony) make an attempt at navigating the subway. It's easy at first, where the stations display signs in English, but veer off the beaten track and you're up there without a paddle. It's a humbling and mind-numbing experience. You could be the most well of well-travelled men, convinced of how much you know the ropes, and all of a sudden you haven't got a clue where the fuck you are. It's not just translation we're on about here, you may as well be a new-born sprog for all you recognize.

We do finally arrive in Akihabra, also known as Electric Town, and then you're in for it. I know there's billions of people upon this land but how many choices of Hoover do you need? Can there be that many flats? Consumer durable freakdown. Watches and cameras and tellies and clocks, in shapes and sizes beyond belief, gadgets and gizmos and God knows what. Its overwhelming and it's intriguing at the same time, but before long it does your head right in. It's too much for Bob, who hails a cab and is out of the place.

Reconvening much later in the hotel bar, lovely design (and at £10 a lager it ought to be), and then it's off to Lexington Queen. Infamous amongst bands who visit Tokyo, this is a club where for selected foreigners almost everything is free, and a proper touch when you're in the world's most expensive city. The deal is, the club invites in overseas bands/artists/models and the like and lays it all on in the hope that the Japanese will want to hang out, and, in the process, spend legions of serious cash. It's odd, I know, but who am I to scoff at an such an offer? As it happens, the drinks on freemans are double weak and you need to drink them by the trayful. But before long there are members of our party jumping through hoops whilst others commandeer the DJ booth, treating all and sundry to never-ending Creation 'whites'. Love Corporation and JBC. Hypnotone and World Unite. As a cushion/sofa war breaks out, horrified punters cling open-mouthed to the walls. Well, I guess that's what they've paid for, and if it was a show they're after …

We're promptly shown the door, not before a minor scuffle, and we're firmly told not to come back, which of course starts a barrage of rubbish such as 'Yeah, well it's a shitty club, anyway', 'Stick it up your arse, mate', and 'We could buy this place, y'know'. Yeah, even that old chestnut.

Why are we here? That's right, there's some work to be done, isn't there? The amazing thing is the show starts at 7 pm. What? Is this a gig for the under fives? We get to Club Quattro and spin some tunes. Tim is on the Arthur Lee and Love tip and my set takes the 'BEEF! How low can you go?' route. The crowd sway gently and fix us smiles. But, tunes aside, it's nigh-on silent and when you compare it to some of the staggering, stumbling, falling and fumbling that goes on in clubs back home it's bizarre to see a place so full of people and yet so motionless, dare I say lifeless. I know it's early, but liven up a bit. Here, pass these T-shirts around, will ya, and everyone suck just under the left sleeve …

'JUST WHAT IS IT YOU WANT TO DO?'
Well that's got them going.
'Bob-bee.' 'Bob-bee.' 'Bob-bee.'
Well, any doubts I had are left at the T-shirt stall – I'm dancing with the rest of 'em and 'Loaded', believe it or not, is even better live. I hadn't been to a gig this exciting for years. This band swagger. Attitude. Arrogance. Physical. Sex. I see and hear Iggy, Sly and the Stones, the Pistols, Shoom and the Clash. Put it together and what have you got? A top night out, that's what you got. I even like the old stuff as well.
What's odd is that despite the crowd obviously loving it, between each song there's a strange silence, save for the odd scream and occasional 'Bob-beeeee'.

Bob-bee sits cross-legged centre-stage, maracas-a-mental like some lunatic guru, lapping it up and loving every minute, with a smile so wide we all fall in. The band wrap a groove round the whole of the night, and they really have carried it off. Encore follows encore until the owners of the building muscle in with keys in hand, shut the gig down and demand the crowd leave. Something about curfews, and in an instant the crowd's gone and we're left to reflect on where we've all been. Also where we're all going, 'cos its only half-eight.

The next night, same place, same time, same vibe, 'cept word's travelled fast and outside there's a welcoming party of screaming girls. Hold on, this isn't the Osmonds. The same faces keep showing up no matter where you roam, hiding behind a tree outside the hotel, and queuing in the café behind you when you go buy a bun. Nothing's said, but you can't move for giggles.

The drinking starts early and tonight's the big game – well, it'll be more like dawn, what with the time difference, and there's many an hour to kill in between. Somehow we find ourselves back at the door of Lexington Queen and, believe it or not, they let us back in. But this time we're not mucking about – me and Innes skip the toy tequilas and purchase champagne. Pomagne more like, but it does the trick, getting you wrecked without laying you out and with nothing else about you need all the help you can get. The sushi bar is top-notch and several of us are busy procuring food tokens from the non-eaters amongst us. I've dreamt about that tuna ever since. Tonight the club is dripping with Glens (Glen Hoddles – models) and it would be very easy to get carried away … but – to the taxis! Much more important things at hand! The World Cup semi-final! Kick-off time approaches back in Turin and tomorrow I am going to Rome!

For some reason my room is selected as the TV room, but I don't care 'cos I'm going to Rome. Believe me, there's no room to swing a cat, but eleven drunk bodies somehow squeeze in, and in a matter of minutes the mini-bar's dry. They're like fucking locusts. Toby sorts it pronto, as he's earlier made a record of where the stockroom is, and we're soon singing our hearts out in a sea of miniatures. Strikes me the room is divided pro-England/pro the Germans but I don't care 'cos *I'mmm … on my way to Ro-ma and I shall not be moved, on my way to …* what's that Gazza crying for … oi! get out the fucking way … *Ro-ma, I shall not be …* Yesssss … Ohhh Gary, Gary – Gary, *Gary, Gary, Gary Lineker … WE'RE ON OUR WAY TO RO-MA, WE SHALL NOT BE …* NOOOOOOOOO! *Deutschland! Deutschland! …* it's like a fucking madhouse in here … *Ohhh Flower of Scot-land … Come on England! Come on England!*

Silence. Bedlam. Silence. Fucking pandemonium. Penalties are evil. Come on Chris WADDLE YOU FUCKING WANKER!!!!!!! NO … NO-OO … What's this lot doing hugging and singing … ON MY BED!! … *DEUTSCHLAND, DEUTSCHLAND ÜBER ALLES* … I'm not having it …

The first glass smashes against the wall and in some infinite wisdom I get out of the room. I have lost it. It's now a rampage. Kicking in doors, punching bins, debris behind me all the way up the hall. I don't wanna hurt anyone but that fucking ice machine has been asking for it all night. Aaaarrrgghhh! Crrraaassshhhh! That's sorted him out.
Back down the hall. Faces duck back terrified behind doors. I'm telling you the lid has definitely flipped.
'Right you lot!'
'Grant, easy.'
GET OUT OF MY FUCKING ROOOOOM!'
The bed went, the bedding went, the chairs went up in the air but after two hours with that lot in there I don't think I actually made that much difference.

By the way, I'm not going to Rome any more.

Where I am going in fact, is to jail. That's if I don't come across with eleven grand more sharpish than sharp. Eleven grand. Can you imagine? I can't even accuse them of doing their sums wrong. They've presented me with a comprehensive report and three pages long it is, too.

Not long after collapsing about 7 am there'd been a rotten

commotion going on in my head. There's no hiding place from the daylight, as the curtains have been pulled clean off the wall (silly move, that), and I can't dive under a pillow because they don't exist. There's a horrible mob trying to break down my door – I know it's the old bill and, although I'm gonna deny the lot of it, the room looks like a bomb's hit it, so you may as well whack on the bangles, judge.

Turns out it's the hotel manager. With the assistant manager. He's with the second assistant manager, and so on, right down to the job-experience kid. Every single one of them is carrying an instamatic and they're more than well keen, this lot. Incredibly, the manager still asks permission to enter, and when I give the okay it's a free-for-all. Apart from the police I suppose, the last thing I need in this room is a dozen jobsworths leaping about, practically fighting each other to take pictures of a scratch, and firing flashes like they're going out of fashion. What I really need is a big fat ice-pack. 'Could anyone please get me some …' It's that moment, that horrible moment when it all starts flooding back. Don't worry about that ice, ta.

Now fair's fair, the gaff is trashed, no denying that. I have been bang out of order and I deserve all I get. But 1500 quid for the door? Four hundred for a fag burn? Two for a scratch? The ice machine's a positive bargain at a couple of grand but as for the rest … It goes on and on. It's a brand new hotel, only open two weeks and something says they're trying to make an example out of me. The biggest joke is the repair of the mark that runs along one wall. Apparently the whole wall has to be replaced so that the colours will match, which'll take a month and put two rooms out of use. Total cost 4000. They're having a laugh. I know many a brickie who'd jump at the chance of a trip to Japan: a monkey in the bin and he'd have it sorted in two days.

Also having a laugh are the collective members of Primal Scream, stood in reception and admiring my woe. I've turned on the tears by this point but they're not far off from being real. It's been a mad old year and it's only half-done, been having girl trouble and consumption's been high. At this moment it feels like it's all coming on top. And the Germans have knocked us out the fucking World Cup.

As the hotel is holding my passport I can't do the hop. The first thing Innes does at the start of any foreign tour is demand the tour manager hand him his air ticket, which he tucks in his passport and keeps upon his person at all times, the theory being, that with this lot, the off may be required at a drop of a hat. Demented Scout, he's always prepared. I see his point. With the luxury of this knowledge he is now also making himself very busy. In fact, he's being a right pest. Obviously still intoxicated by the English defeat (something about 800 years of oppression and all that – he's a proper Willie Wallace, this bloke), and a breakfast I'd bet was liquid alone, he is well involving himself in negotiations. We're informed the ice machine has been mortally wounded and a replacement has already been ordered in. Innes tells the manager to wrap it up to go. The manager is not impressed. He's got a face like a brick wall. A very high one. I doubt there's a ladder high enough.

The luckiest break for me is when the head man of Smash, the promoters, turns up, having been summoned by the boss of the hotel chain, which also happens to be part of one of the biggest and most powerful corporations in Japan. The big men have already threatened to close his operation down, sack the tour and send the lot of us home. Oh dear – Creation will be impressed. Reports filtering back that Primal Scream are smashing the gaff up would come of no great surprise. But their own employee? Thinking about it, they probably loved it. The irony is it's Mr Summer of Love of the anti-rock 'n' roll alliance who's up before the beak. Half-a-dozen eggs on my face or what?

Well, despite the pressure he's obviously under, Masahiro from Smash puts up a fight on my behalf. I've never met the man before, but he gets stuck right in. He hates the corporate world as much as the rest of us, and apart from Michael Mansfield, QC, a better advocate in this life I couldn't wish for. The Scream are now telling him to book a gig, a benefit gig, to cover the damage. There's good causes and lost causes, but what on earth do you put on a poster for this one? 'Save the trouser press'? Their offer is a generous one, though, and, as I've only known them for a relatively short time, quite a surprising one. But they feel they played a part, and a lot of the (admittedly minor) peripheral damage had been done even before I had my funny turn, and now the counting's being done they're standing up.

Time doesn't actually allow to squeeze another show in so it's back to the negotiating table. Masa strikes a deal that involves two grand down, return of passport then three instalments, three Gs a go, wired monthly from the UK. Well, I settle for that and there's just about enough cash in the T-shirt kitty to cover the initial. I have to sign a promise form, though I reckon they've got two hopes of getting the rest, Bob Hope and no hope. Masa agrees with me.

What do I learn from this little event?

Curtains cost a fortune in Japan.
As do chairs, doors and plasterers.
Masa is a top man.
I shop at Do-It-All-In.
Wobblers are expensive.
Chris Waddle should weigh me in.

Soul II Soul are in town and we meet up at an after-show party, but after last night's palaver at the Creston Hotel I'm keeping my head well down and my tail tucked firmly between my legs.

By comparison the rest of the tour is quiet, but the gigs just get better and better. I've also been roped in to tune the guitars, but I don't mind 'cos it gets me near. This is some band; I wish I was up there with them. Best I can do is slip on during the encore with the rest of the crew and march about barmy with a tambourine.

Tokyo. Osaka. Nagoya. Four hundred miles and you'd never know. The bullet train flies. Wicked ice cream served up by a stewardess. Beats curly cheese on British Rail. The cities never end. The buildings just shrink 'til they reach some paddies and then they start to rise again. It's a fascinating place, that's for sure, but nobody's too upset when the tour is done. The back page of the itinerary has a simple entry: 'Back to life, Back to reality.' Just about sums it up.

My performance aside, I have to say all the warnings I'd had turned out to be tosh: Primal Scream had behaved impeccably. Polite as pussycats. They did the job, very well at that. Then someone said it wouldn't be the same anywhere else. Nowhere has a drug drought quite like Japan …

Oh yeah. Pictures. I happened to take a few of the band on this trip. Not for any other reason than I had my camera around (the one I found during the Poll Tax riots. Thanks Maggie, that one's on you. Enterprise culture and all that). I had no desire to be a rock smudger. Demos, elections and the odd war was much more my thing (the great British photo-journalist Don McCullin's my man) but as Japan was a new one on me I thought I'd take a few snaps. I'd barely picked up a camera since a trip to Central America a couple of years before, as some of the things I saw in Salvador and Nicaragua burnt right through my brain, plus, of course, the house of acid came along. So I was more than chuffed that when, on our return, the band saw what I'd shot and wanted to use them for press and promo. Nice way to reduce the room-damage debt as well. That's where this book began. No plan, no pre-meditation, it just grew as we went along and as more and more shots appeared. The day me and Bobby got talking about Pennie Smith's great photographic document, 'Before and after the Clash', we knew we were on.

The band returned to the studio, as there was an album to do, but not before the video for 'Come Together' was shot, though. Literally mobs appeared at the shoot at Orinoco Studios in south-east London, many of whom bore gifts, and a proper little party we had, too. That's us leaping about with the band in the vid. The likes of Sheertaft, Alex Nightingale, Si Stevens, Kazza P. E'd up and playing pass the poppers. We might just as well have been at a rave.

There was Madonna at Wembley, where me and Bob tried holding our own on the dancing front, which is a difficult task when you're surrounded by gangs of feisty fourteen-year-olds gyrating in bra tops, giving it attitude when any bloke walks by. Proper intimidation. The Material Girl has released the piranhas. About time. Over the years we've asked for it, so I suppose we deserve all we get.

8 September. Unforgettable night at Jam Studios in Finsbury Park, where the bulk of *Screamadelica* was recorded. I pull plenty of favours in my Creation hat, and with the help of my new flatmate Kaz and the Stevens Simon, lay on a party to raise some cash for Great Ormond Street children's hospital. Danny Rampling, Steve Lee, Glen Gunner on the decks, the Scream in full attendance and Freddie Guarana sitting at the front door handing the guests Guarana punch served from a black plastic bin. By the look of things I don't think many are paying attention to his 'Drugs are for mugs' flyers, but it was a nice try. What a night!

Earlier in the day though, mad Roy Pollard, who ran the Aquarius parties, fell from the (very high) ceiling while putting up drapes. I thought he was dead. Broke his neck at least. Thankfully, it was nothing so bad, but he was carted off to hospital, which dampened the proceedings. But at about 1 am he came flying into the main room, big smile beaming, and dancing on crutches. A-ha, such was the spirit of the times … Having a laugh and raising three grand.

22 November. She's gone. She's gone. That evil bitch is gone. Bye bye Maggie and rot in hell. But why did it take another seven years to rid ourselves of the rest of that shower?

The end of the year sees me leaving Creation. I started to lose faith in the dance scene. It got too much . Twenty-four seven. Which wouldn't have been a problem if it had been worth fighting for, but the more involved I got the more I realized people were losing sight of the possibilities. Corrupted by moolah, getting drunk on the power. Superstar DJs. Rock 'n' roll all over again. That's not what it was supposed to be about. I handed in my notice, beat a retreat and went off to find the Gulf War.

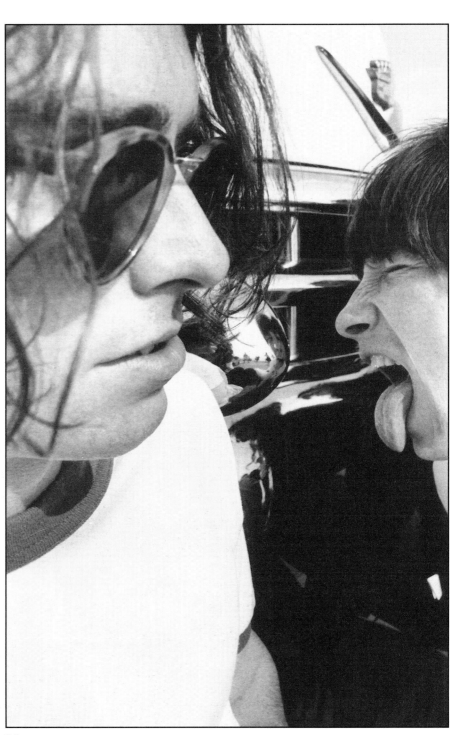

Brighton.

Electric Town. Bob and Tony Martin. Tokyo.

Above Osaka Station.
Below The Bullet Train. Japan.

Above Club Quattro. Nagoya. Japan.
Below left Andrew Innes, **right** Toby Toman. 'Come together' video. Orinoco studios. London.

'Come together' video. Orinoco studios. London.

1991

One of the greatest albums ever made?

It is for me, matey. With an arm twisted up my back and forced to make a decision it's the one I'd pack as a desert island disc. Slip it in a holdall with a bag of doves, ounce of weed and a bottle of rum. Ho ho ho. Half a dozen walnut whips. You'd never see me again.

Jordan closed its border with Syria to foreign nationals after a French photographer had been stabbed covering an anti-West demo in Amman. That stumped me. The only way into Iraq was via eastern Jordan and that border was opening one minute, closing the next. Stuck in Damascus, I hung out a while but got sick of being followed by men in odd raincoats. The long hair of the time didn't help either.

We're a few months into the year before *Screamadelica* begins to take shape. The Primal Scream approach to recording could be classed as unorthodox, unpredictable or anarchic. Certainly narcotic. It can drive the record company mad but the fact is, if it's worth it, it's worth waiting for. Appearing gradually in bits and bobs, those who get to hear it unanimously agree – this band are off their fucking tits.

How about a little taster then? So they give us 'Higher Than The Sun'. Stop it. You can't do that to people; they have to go to work in the morning. This isn't a single, it's a grand fucking opus.

The first attempt to shoot a video for this record follows the title just a little too literally. Talk about go wild in the country. It never got shown. The out-takes? Give the Stones' 'Cocksucker Blues' a U certificate, will ya?

The Hammers go out in the semi-final after a trouncing from Forest, featuring a narky young bastard by the name of Roy Keane. That was never a sending-off, ref! Tony Gale walked and we went out of the FA Cup. Mind you, you had to pity the Forest. Subdued in victory, as the sound of east London drowns Villa Park. 'Billy Bonds' claret-and-blue army.' Again. And again. And again. Throughout the second half. Every time they scored it got louder. Balloons and smiles. A complete lack of aggro. *The ICF in fancy dress*! Even Cloughie stood up and cheered. Something happened that day – a new way of thinking. The very same fans who had, in the eighties, created a fashion out of hooliganism, in one afternoon made hooliganism look unfashionable. Ecstasy may well have had something to do with it. It's a full two years before *Fever Pitch*. Never mind Baddiel, New Chelsea, Zoë Ball and the rest of the 'football is the new rock 'n' roll' brigade. (Preston away. Pissing it down. Where were you?)

For the 'Higher' cover I'm asked to take pictures of a painting by

Paul Cannell. This bloke is a genius, just like Salvador Dali in fact. A painter, a genius and a complete nutcase. He sent the canvas over but it wasn't quite dry. You should have heard the cabbie curse, 'That's fucking ruined my shirt, that has, and what's it s'posed to be anyway, looks like the cunt was sick on it.' You're probably not wrong, mate.

Denise Johnson has become involved with the band as a backing vocalist, which can only be good. We'd worked together with Hypnotone on Creation, and she'd set Electronic and A Certain Ratio singles alight ('Won't Stop Loving You', a masterpiece) and it was a pleasure to do business with her. Soul sister number one. She joins Bob, Innes and the Throb (you want to know why they call him the Throb? Oh, use your head) on a June Friday night in Soho. We do a little photo shoot. More time in the pub than on the streets but that's all right, we're having fun. We bump into a crowd just out from the *Rocky Horror* stage show. Haven't these people got any friends who could have a word? The world of camp is a joy to behold but berks up from Bromley in fishnet tights really is not a pretty sight. Bobby grabs a feather boa, just for a couple of shots. The bloke it belongs to is having kittens. Don't get out your pram, mate.

You could say the same to me a couple of weeks later when we're coming back in the early hours from a warm-up gig at the Irish Centre in Northampton. We're in a twelve-seater van, but it's more like a mobile zoo. I don't know how many are in the back there and quite frankly I don't care 'cos I got my seat, but I get the hump when people fall from the darkness and land in my lap. Especially when we're doing a ton. And I'm driving.

This gives me second thoughts about doing the driving on the forthcoming UK tour. I like a bit of a cavort just like the rest of 'em, but I'm really not the best spectator in the world. If I can't get involved I'd rather not be there, but this has to be overcome as there's merchandising to take care of, and by driving at least I'm always with the band, which for pictures is good.

The tour turns out to be totally exhausting. Driving all day. T-shirt stall set up. Grab a bite. Doors open 8 o'clock. Man the stand 'til 2 am, maybe 3. At times it's mental, like first day of the sales. Post-midnight you're lucky to see a soul – they're all off their nut, backstage and out front. Show me someone who isn't, and I'll show you a copper. I feel like the kid in short trousers outside the pub. It's all right when I can set up in the hall, then I can have it up on the table but it's frustrating when it's all going off and I'm stuck peering through the double doors. Occasionally, I'll get relieved by Simon Stevens or one of the crew, and get the opportunity to shoot a few frames, but more often than not they're charging about as well.

Once I'm packed away I can join in the hank, but there's a hell of a lot of catching up to do. Besides, within a few hours I'll be back at the wheel of the ambulance. It may as well be, the state of some of the bodies strewn daily across the floor behind me. Looks like it was a nasty accident.

The shape of the band has changed again, which, apart from the ever-present trio of Gillespie, Innes and Young, it is wont to do from time to time. Denise is on board. Henry and Toby too. New signings are: on programming duty, Hugo Nicholson, ex-Bocca Juniors, and studio spar of Andrew Weatherall, and, let me introduce to you, the one and only Martin Duffy. Mar-tin Du-foir, on keys, piano and Guinness. Loads of it. The Spanish have a saying for people like him, '*No hay dos*', meaning there aren't two. Thank Christ for that. Another, and we really wouldn't be able to cope. He can't half tinkle the ivories though. The first gig is a home one for him, the Birmingham Institute in Digbeth. It really kicks off. Indie dance? And the rest. Duff has a whale and the last time I see him he's eating plants back at the Campanile Hotel. Douglas Hart is around, shooting the movie. Now a film-maker, he goes back to the Jesus & Mary Chain days, playing the bass while Bob G banged the drum.

The shows are, of course, structured around the Scream onstage but it's not the sum total of the night. Not by a long shot. DJs open and close and if you pay through the doors you certainly get your money's worth. With on-tour DJs Andrew Weatherall and Alex Paterson from the Orb, supplemented by the likes of Justin Robertson in Manchester and the Slam crew in Glasgow, you've also got the cream of the UK scene. Quality night out.

The Scream have connections with Manchester that go back a long way, and most of them like a bit of a party. As a result, the dressing room at the Hacienda is as full as Old Trafford, and you'd need to find a tout to get you in. Word is, backstage passes are going for a tenner a time.

Glasgow is home. From home. The families of Scream turn out. Proud as peacocks. So they should be, it's the gig of the tour, in a beautiful crumbling old ballroom that I bet has seen some right old do's. But the energy in the Plaza tonight reaches dangerous levels. Heart-attack material. It'll blow up in a minute if this lot doesn't calm down. What a crowd – always been the same in Glasgow. Back on the old Sham 69 tours it was the same, the place we all looked forward to. Absolutely mental. Nothing's changed. What do they put in the water up there?

Bottle it, mate, bottle it.

One of the promoter's pals has laid on an aftershow at a flat over near the Gorbals. Deary deary me, there's some naughty tablets in town and whatever's left over from the gig have ended up here. Gobble, gobble, gobble.

'Anyone seen Smiler?'

The whole house stood up.

We've lost Tafty. The grifter of Greenock. AKA Sheertaft of Creation classic 'Cascades' fame. Been mates with the band for years. I'm sure he turned up with us.

The Duff reads poems in the kitchen. Sorry, shouts poems. Sat under the T-shirt stall earlier writing them on the back of a poster. The enchanted children gather round the pilled-piper. They haven't got a clue what he's on about. You think he does? Amazingly, yes. Another genius. People are in fits. There's a book in that boy. Either that or they should throw it at him.

We've found Tafty. He's still alive. You wouldn't think so by looking at him. Bombed out, he's made his way down three of the

floors all right, it's just the last one that seems to have been the problem. The man lays in a pool of bodily fluids, every one you can think of and a few you can't. We'd better get this boy home. Too buzzed to taxi, though. March of the mad stares …

Thrash, the other half of the Orb, popped up to the first gig. He's still here. Hasn't slept or changed his clothes and we're four days in. The crew have issued an ultimatum: sort those rotten trainers out. Banned from the bus 'til you do. He obviously doesn't want to go home yet because he duly dumps the offending articles in the nearest bin and marches off up the road barefooted. He looks like the wild man of Borneo. The RSPCA have been called. They can send over their yeti net. It's a bit dusty.

The people of Nottingham run for cover. He's last seen in the high street, in Clarks. 'Excuse me, love, do you sell shoes?'

There's murders back at the Post House Hotel. Some liggers-come-dealers up from the smoke. Wankers taking liberties, the kind of rubbish you don't want around. There's a bit of damage, nothing to write home about, but enough to earn the band a ban from the Post House chain.

I've done myself in here. Got a bunch of pictures as suggestions for the upcoming album cover. Nice stuff shot at the Angus Cameron-directed video for 'Don't Fight It, Feel It'. Something else has been developing, though. While shooting Paul Cannell's painting for 'Higher' I'd also picked out some details here and there, to give a choice. One of the details became the cover of the remix. It was a mad, abstract face. Mark Dennis the dark menace was in charge of marketing at Creation and for some ads he changed the colours in the face to primary: red, yellow, blue, black, white. Looked amazing. I immediately had to do T-shirts like that.

Alan McGee turned up in Cambridge that Friday. We had a meet at the hotel and discussed the pictures for the cover. I'm buzzed. Then he came to the gig. Came over to the T-shirt stall. 'Yes! *That's* the fucking sleeve, man.'

'What?'

'That red T-shirt!'

Well, how could you argue? It was, and is, a brilliant cover, and probably the last great vinyl sleeve of all time. Rest that record right next to *Sgt Pepper's*. History. Before records shrunk. When the revolution comes we should march into town waving flags of red with that face on them. It'd take a nation of millions … Anyhow, I'm proud enough to have a picture on the gatefold. Pleased as punch if the truth be known, to this day and forever more. Album of our times. I'm on board. Cannell too. You can't argue with that.

The Orb rocks an aftershow party at the Junction Club and, predictably, it's a messy affair. The travelling-party entourage is growing by the day. It's the weekend and it seems all roads have led to Cambridge. Thrash is wearing his new shoes in on the dancefloor and Tafty's clothes have dried out. We're going to need a *fleet* of ambulances by the end of all this.

This is going on day after day with not a day off in between. Conventional wisdom says Primal Scream cannot have a day off. If they do, that's when there's trouble. With a lot more time on their hands, they'll *really* get fucked up and it may take days to find them. I have to add here that this doesn't apply to the whole of the touring party. Henry is happy with the odd glass of wine and Denise doesn't even smoke, but if you're looking for candidates for the temperance society I'm afraid that's the very best I can do, so it's back to back all the way. We may lose some along the way, but in war there are casualties. Just make sure you've got your helmet on. The gigs don't seem to suffer, though, but could anyone tell? Sometimes we have to lend the audience our ambulance it gets so bad.

Just like the sixties. If you were there – you weren't there.

After yet another space ride through the night I'm trying to face up to the longest day. Norwich to Bristol, 220 miles east to west and the roads aren't good. Only thing in our favour is it's a Sunday. Well, not much of the day left, time we get everyone together. I'm not the only one – everybody's bombed. We might have trouble making this one. It's another nuisance convention in the back of the van. Alex Nightingale, hyper-mental son of DJ Annie and one of the band's pals from Brighton, is wrapped in tape and at one point Duffy has driven me so mad –
'Grant.'
'What, Duff?'
'Grant.'
'What?'
'Grant.'
'*What*? Duff.'
'Grant.'
'SHUT THE FUCK UP!!!'
— I'm struggling to throw him out the door as we're going along the motorway. I find him later at a service station clutching five litres of oil and a cuddly toy.

We make it, of course we do. Just … They play a gig and I set up the stall and it seems only minutes before we're back in the van – no hotel in Bristol but a drive back to London. Andrew Weatherall is not into it, throws a moody, demands some cash and takes the train. I wish I could.
Time I get everyone back it's 6 am and I'm practically dead. We've been away one week. The inside of the van looks like a council tip – smells like one too. The things I find I'd rather not try to describe. It's scarred me for life.

The tour's not over, there's a gig that night, and a glorious one it is, too. Leicester Square is buzzing and big money is changing hands. The Empire is rammo and we all lose weight. I'll give you an example of what the audience is like: a bloke approaches the T-shirt stall, eyes very far in the back of his head. He notices the sun-face shirt. 'ONE OF THEM!' he cries, laughing like he's found the pot at the rainbow's end.
'That'll be seven pounds please, mate.'
After searching every pocket at least a couple of times, he discovers a tenner and hands it over. I give him the shirt and three pound coins.
The most puzzled look explodes across his face. He looks at the shirt. He looks at the change. He looks quickly again at the shirt. At the change. Then, with a face full of worry, he looks at me.
'What's this for, mate?'

I'm pissing myself so much by this point I have to retreat for fear of freaking him out any more. And he wasn't even the bloke who came in wearing a Thunderbirds suit.

Inevitably there's a party, it's the end of the tour. Thrown together by the Kinky Disco crew. I'm so done in I give it a miss; I've just about had enough. There's only so much you can pour down your neck unless you want to end up in the madhouse. Instead, I retire at dawn to the Dallas Diner, an all-night cafe at Smithfield Market accompanied by co-workers and flat-mates Kazza P and Marty the lights. He was the legend behind World Unite, doing the parties in '88, another stalwart from Creation Dance. An egg, a bean and a

chip. A big mug of tea. Let the dust settle. Get my head together. Got to be at *The Face* to deliver pictures this afternoon. Then to Europe with the House of Love. I am fucked.

Bobby, too, has an appointment that afternoon to meet the world's press in the Hilton Hotel. His companion is Monsieur Dufoir. Course they haven't slept – until they reach the press conference. Duffy is out like a light. He bursts into life on two occasions and says all there is that needs to be said. Bobby is getting bombarded by journos all shouting at once. The Duff leaps to his feet: 'WHY DON'T YOU LOT LET YOUR FUCKING EARS DO THE FUCKING TALKING!' Slumps back across the table.

Question after question about drugs, drugs, drugs. Bobby is barely conscious. Someone mentions addiction. Duffy slowly rises: 'Do you know you can get addicted to wallpaper?'

Put that in a book of quotes.

I get to Geneva and sleep at last, and for a whole day. Except it's on a bed of feathers and finally my body caves in. My back has gone. I am now horizontal. Spend the duration of a garden party staring at the sky – not on anything, either. Carried out. This is post-Scream stress disorder, surely. I'm going to sue the bastards.

In need of recuperation I slip off to Tenerife to spend my birthday with my girlfriend. It's all going off in the clubs of Playa de las Americas, which is great for a night out but it's a bit home from home (Bethnal Green-on-Sea). We chill elsewhere. The DJs love the white labels I've taken out, the infamous unmarked 'scat' mix of 'Don't Fight It, Feel It', that had them all guessing for a while. The dance fraternity were going crazy for this tune, but didn't have a clue who it was. You could have got a ton a piece at one stage, such was the demand. A great rave goes off in the Cactus Park, I'm back on my feet and dancing by this point, and a Frankie Knuckles 'Your Love' says it all.

We've got a few bits and bobs left when it's time to leave. Walk in the airport and who should we bump into, just off the plane from London? I kid you not, it's Andrew Innes and a posse from Manchester. Gagging for an up. Lucky they met us then. Lucky for us, too. That's how off our heads we were at the time. Stood there doing deals in the arrivals hall of an international airport.

September 1991. *Screamadelica*. If you don't own this record I have only one question: 'Why not?'

October. It's Japan again. The band's status is rising high. Bigger gigs, more gigs, for one of which they are donating their fee to the Creston Hotel fund. Yes, they are keeping their word. I hadn't kept mine. Well, not the promise I'd signed last year. Big corporation? Bah. I knocked them. Didn't hear another word and thought they had left it – had they, hell. One day the offices of Smash are invaded by all sorts of legal paramilitaries and Masahiro is forced to hand over the outstanding – that or immediate eviction. He had no choice, but cool as he is, chose not to make a big song and dance about it. It only came to light when Mick Griffiths, the band's agent at the time, found out from another source. So a gig has been slotted in for the purpose of squaring it all up. I can only offer my humble thanks. Right. Can we get satellite in this hotel? The Hammers have got Coventry at home. Oh, don't go. That won't be an expensive one, honest. That's only a grand at tops. Oh, come back.

I'm gonna make a complaint to reception. There never seems to a ice machine on my floor.

The lobby is awash with the teeny patrol. Should Bobby G emerge from the lift pandemonium breaks out, except all these girls run in the opposite direction, giggling and screaming. With an approach akin to feeding the lions they nervously edge back, closing in slowly, until the lesser-spotted moptop is surrounded. It doesn't take long; he's soon down, stoned to death with a thousand tiny presents. All exquisitely wrapped, and surely worth a fortune, the contents include an amazing box of … peanuts … biscuits (feed that boy up, he doesn't look like he's had a decent meal in months). A couple of pencils, boxer shorts with a delightful cherry-tomato imprint, a gonk (Bobby looks like he wants to rip it's head off. You never know, made in Thailand and all that). Still, it's the thought that counts.

These girls are by no means groupies in the conventional sense, neither after a line, nor offering a blow. (No one's interested anyway: too busy going mental all the time to worry about girls.) Conversely, they hardly speak, which is kinda difficult anyway when you're covering your face with your hand the whole time, and they certainly don't seem to want to touch, being more than happy just to be near. That's knicker-wetting happy, by the way some are standing. Pictures are taken and then they're gone, hysterically rushing out the front door and squeezing into cabs. It all appears quite strange, until after a couple of days a pattern emerges. When we get to the station to take the train to the next city they'll be there on the platform to see us off. More peanuts and gonks, then they'll wave and run off. So sweet. Three hours later you disembark the train and, oh look, it's our friends again. Brilliant, I'm getting to like those peanuts. The reality is, they follow every footstep the band make, having hotels and transport worked out in advance and I wonder where they get the bugs bunny. Still, when you're in love you find it, don't you?

I never had any great amount of cash when I was their age, but that never stopped me doing the length and breadth of Britain and across the continent in pursuit of the Jam, Sham and West Ham. (Hang on, why do I always go for names ending in am? The Scream … oh no, voodoo! Even bleedin' temazepam – what's happening here? Where will it all end? Tottenham? No, no chance. Thinking about it, I used to love spam as well when I was a kid and I fucking hate the stuff now.)

Mind you, I reckon it's a lot harder to jib in Japan and the hectors on the train won't leave you alone, checking tickets at every stop. Everybody even obeys the Green Cross Man in this country so I doubt that this lot are up to tricks. Must be loaded then.

I notice it with the T-shirts as well. Some of these kids will come in and buy one of everything. Some who haven't even got tickets will turn up at the door, literally beg to be let in and still buy something. What on earth must it have been like for the Beatles? I dread to think. We're fast running out of anything with the name Primal Scream on it as it is, and they're even putting in offers for the cardboard boxes it came in. I have to radio base and send for reinforcements. Freighting and its customs formalities will take too long; the only way is someone flying over and hand-delivering. Before you know it, my pal Kevin Bridgey is packing his bags full of T-shirts. There's a fuck-up at Heathrow, with minutes to go before departure, and between him and our two girlfriends they've only got enough for a single. Aeroflot, the Russian airline, won't accept a kite, advise him to take the single and purchase the return, same price, in Japan. This would later cause no end of grief, but it's nice seeing Kevin at Narita airport, yesterday's papers tucked under his arm (oh, the joy of a decent read), poor bloke can hardly walk under the weight of the dickie dirts. He'd had a grilling but hadn't cracked and at this stage it looks like a good deal for all of us. The band are restocked, I'm pleased to have been able to give him the trip and,

being a DJ besides, he's brought his box, which is just as well for what is to come.

What comes first is that finally, and begrudgingly, I have to hand over £880 for a single back to London for him, after countless rows with Aeroflot in both Tokyo and London. They've tucked us up. Same price, my foot. I take it out on the traffic, charge screaming across the busiest square in Tokyo, Shibuya Cross, the one where the *Bladerunner* buildings run ads on huge screens. I'm armed with no more than a complimentary Tobu Hotel see-through woman's umbrella, Kevin is struggling to keep up and the local population run for cover. I've gone again, haven't I? Maybe it's just this place. It's so claustrophobic. Walls that talk to you. People that don't. They pass you by as if you weren't there. Where's the emotion? Where's the space? Where's the air?

A trip to Mount Fuji with guitar tech Jason should sort me out. But even when we get up there it's covered in cloud. Solace is found in a tiny jazz club in Osaka where we all go and chill out to a beautiful set from Astrud Gilberto, the girl from Ipanema. Sweetness.

Connie Yee, Japan's No.1 dance-music promoter, called it Japan's first bona-fide rave. Tomo Hirata from dance mag *Remix* agreed. It went right off, mate. I've been to a few raves in my time, but this one is up there with the best of them. Sunrise. Energy. Biology. No drugs, either. Well, that's a bit of a porky, actually. There were a few bits and pieces about but I'd say we'd got the bulk of 'em. It was just one of those nights when it all falls into place. A crowd that is totally up for it, a band without equals, with songs that make your spirits soar. Higher than the sun, way into the next solar system and beyond. A pulsating, mating love groove. *Pump it up!* This is the BOLLOCKS!! There's one or two bug-eyed Westerners in attendance, having it as ever, but it really looks like the Japanese have caught on. What a difference a year makes.

I must add that this was no ordinary gig. After a week on the road the tour winds up with a mini-residency at Club Citta in Kawasaki, a satellite town of Tokyo, though in this country everywhere's a satellite town of Tokyo. There's been three gigs of the normal kind (even those had been raucous enough), but on the last day after the earlier show the doors opened again at midnight. It's the perfect venue. Holds about 1200, scaffolding banking the back wall where the DJ, sound and lights operate from, a big high square room for the visuals to run wild in, and a slightly raised tier at the back and along one side that serves as a natural dance platform. Admittedly, it's a more clubby crowd that bounce through the door, but we rocked the gaff. DJ Richie from Expansions opens and gets the place going. The Scream come on about 2 am, and, playing in front of two huge 'sun' backdrops, the band are nothing short of magnificent. Cooking with gas. Uproar in the house.

A western hippy type had crept backstage, via Goa, and was doling out the Amsterdam Es. Dynamite. The kind you'd almost forgotten about. Kevin hits the decks and plays a blinder. The band's equipment is packed away and most of our entourage occupy the stage for a little private one. With one move Simon Stevens takes one curtain, I grab the other and we run, pulling them open and revealing all to the hall. The crowd go bananas and many join us up there. Coming together, that's about right. It's around now it becomes a blur as I rush my way to the stars, but at one point I do remember Kevin high above us dancing on top of the speakers, as the security beg him to come down. The stack is wobbling all over the shop but the man is oblivious. Plus, he's been doing it for years. If you ever lost him at a party you only had to look up. Speakers, lighting tower, roof. There he'd be, gurning away. He's *Dances With Wolves* that one. Two Eyes Rolling.

Dai, our tour manager from Smash the promoter, is looking worried. The place is out of control. A party the likes of which is unheard of in Japan. The hall staff are very nervous: it's way past curfew. The army are encircling Tokyo. Scream personnel and punters alike have scaled the scaffolding at the back and it looks like it we could be here for days. Where's that Goa-head when you need her? I try to placate the management with 'just one half-hour more, I promise'. (I'm terrible with promises in Japan.) It's finally closed down when we're wrestled from the decks just before 6 am. What a night. To this day, it's still one of the best I've spent with this band. And there have been a few.

Back at the hotel, which is conveniently around the corner, we colonize a banqueting suite, the blaster comes out and we carry on. Bodies strew the carpet as Duffy sits at a piano in the corner playing the Benny Hill theme. Don't ask me how I packed, or how a couple of hours later we found ourselves at Tokyo airport. Of the flight home, I know nothing. I search frantically for the luggage tag on my bag at Heathrow. How else am I going to find out where I live?

It's ritual time. The one where I know I'm home. No matter where I've been, or for how long, and without wishing to insult the amazing food I've usually sampled, the first thing on the agenda is get down the shop, get the milk, the bread, some beans and a bit of cheese in, toast it up, knock it on top, have a proper brew (especially if you've been to the States. They haven't got a clue about tea that lot. It's got to be boiling, mate!) and I'm away. *Independent* open, eyes down, look in. Bliss.

That's literally all there's time for. There's some ragged faces boarding the bus at 7 o'clock the next morning. Another British tour. Thankfully I'm not driving on this one, though in exchange I've got something I like even less. Nearly two weeks on a tour bus. I don't like them, don't like being trapped, especially with the rock 'n' roll careerists about. Bores me senseless. 'D'you remember when we had to carry that twenty-two-mile truss 144 floors up to the Top Rank, Pontypridd? And then the fucking stage was too small. Ohh, and what about that awful load-out in Winnepeg on the Foreigner tour? Useless local crew. Bunch of peasants, the lot of 'em. If I had been the TM on that tour I'd have …' I can't handle all that. Teddy Bedwards.

In fact, it's all getting a bit showbiz now, bigger trucks, bigger production, bigger crew. Two sleeper coaches, one band, one crew – though thankfully with this band these boundaries are rarely respected. If you end up on the other bus you sleep where you lie. They're not precious about all that: if you're on the firm, you're on the firm, though that can equally be a bit tough on Denise, being the only female in the house and that's just what it is, a house on wheels. Looking at it, I wouldn't want a bunch of madmen back round my gaff every night. Due to the success and incredible critical acclaim of *Screamadelica*, there's also all kinds of rubbish crawling out from under stones and flocking round the band. It's the sycophants' tea-party.

Of course, this happens to all bands to a lesser or greater degree once they break a certain level, but with the reputation the Scream have, it's not hard to imagine some of the pond-life that appears. Sometimes when you're so engulfed by it, you also become blind to it. I know that from when I was in a band, you become intoxicated by the success, addicted to the attention. It's hard to see right from wrong. Some get lost. You have to reserve judgement and see how people come out of it the other side. I take a step aside and get on with my T-shirts.

On this tour I don't think I took one single picture, just tried to chill and listen to the music. Andrew Weatherall, the Orb and Craig Walsh provide the sounds. Tune of the tour? Bassheads' 'Is There Anybody Out There?' Future Sound of London's 'Papua New Guinea'. Neck and neck to the wire.

In fact, I'm not happy on this tour and think about chucking it in. Still, this is personal, and most people in the audience certainly are enjoying themselves, except for one night in Birmingham, which really pissed me off. The band had started to attract a younger audience as well as the mad-eyes, and on this night in particular, there's some really sweet young lads, no more than thirteen, who come to the T-shirt stall, buy their shirts and proudly whip them straight on their backs. The band are due on at 10.30 and their dads'll be back at midnight. You should have seen how excited these kids were. That's me that is, just before the Faces came on back in '72. It means the world to you.

Now I don't know exactly what happened but I don't think it takes a lot of working out: the band are late. Very late. They're never early, but this is beyond reason. People are leaving to catch buses. I love the way Primal Scream refuse to play the corporate-rock game – the unpredictability lends excitement – but this is taking the piss. Those little blokes' eyes when their old men pulled them out nearly had me in tears. The least I could do was bung them some swag and refund their tickets out of the merch money, but I could see nothing was going to make up for missing that gig. Get it together people. Getting caned is one thing, but sometimes you've got to just stop and think.

What with being cooped up on the bus and the ongoing T-shirt wars on the streets with the Manc bootlegging firms, this tour drove me mad, and brilliant as the band can be, I can't see me being around for much longer.

Bob and Steph. 'Don't Fight it' video. London.

Above The Throb. **Below left** Bob. 'Don't Fight it' video. London.
Below right Henry Olsen on the vibes. Recording *Screamadelica*. Jam Studios. London.

The Manager. 'Higher Than The Sun' video.

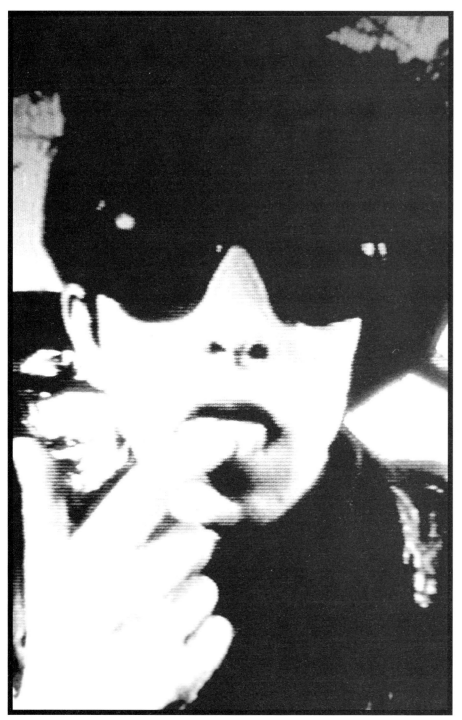

'Higher Than The Sun' video.

Above Come together. Plaza Ballroom. Glasgow.
Below Empire Leicester Square. London.

Above and **Below** Club Citta. Kawasaki. Japan.

Left The Duff. **Right** Andrew Weatherall. On the road. UK.

Left Mornin'. Bob helps Throb to the ambulance. Manchester.
Right Soho. London.

Waiting for the pub to open. Dawn in Glasgow.

Above 365-days-a-year party people. Glasgow.
Below Bob and Alan McGee. Birmingham.

1992

Well, it can't be all bad, can it? Tantrum's over. I've calmed down a bit, had a good sleep, a decent scrub-up and a bit of dinner and I'm raring to go. Where? Amsterdam. Fuck me, you don't half pick 'em, Nightingale. It's his first gig as the band's agent. What a place to start the year and a European tour. People will end up bloody hurting themselves.

The night before we fly (no pun intended), it's over to Wembley to perform the new single, 'Movin' On Up' on Channel Four's *The Word*, particularly memorable for Andrew's superb virtuoso demented kangaroo act. He's leaping about like a man let loose. The camera can't keep up with him. Nor can the band. Phoarr, see that fur coat go! Cutting a dash like Bonnie Prince Charlie. No, that's wrong. Bonnie Prince Berwick, that's it. You wanna ease up, boy.

It's an excellent show at the Paradiso in Amsterdam the next night, and it appears half of London nightlife have turned up to witness it. Paul Oakenfold is over to DJ as well, so how can you go wrong? One night in Oz that bloke changed my life. He reckons this gig in Amsterdam was the one that changed *his* life. Well, at least his DJ life. After throwing his bags in the hotel he headed, with the rest of the posse, to the nearest coffee shop. Where not a lot of coffee actually gets drunk. Paul swears he'll never do it again. Got taught a big lesson. Not before the gig. Why? 'I couldn't string two records together.' He's still the guv'nor.

On the other dates it's a new face out of Brighton by the name of Dino Psaras, young and feisty and handy on the decks. Sixteen years old and loving every minute. Some years later, he emerges as a leading light and top DATman on the Goa trance scene. Amsterdam being Amsterdam drug use is excessively high, and that is just the locals before we get there. No one needs their arm twisted and it's a case of 'when in Rome …', but the problem is, some people seem to forget they've already said it once and just keep on repeating themselves. Some amongst us end up in some terrible states. Take the girl who's tagging along, an English chick, from where I don't know and I don't know who knows her. She's well off her face. There's a banging techno club on a barge and to enter you have to negotiate a tiny, rickety bridge that would be difficult enough in daylight, but this is the middle of the night – SPLASSSHHH! Oh fuck, she's gone in. It's not funny. She's fallen between the quay and the boat. It's January and bitterly cold. She's gone clean through the ice. She won't last long. We struggle to keep hold of her, soundman Oz gets a good grip and yanks her up but it still isn't over, as her glass eye comes bobbing out of her head! It's enough to sober you up. The shock to my system is bad enough; I dread to think what it's done to hers. Seemingly, nish. We've dragged her out and called for coats. She just makes to continue over the bridge as though what had just happened was part of the entry detail. Carries right on into the club. She's just cheated death! She should be checked for

hypothermia and stuck in front of the nearest fire. Instead, by the time we follow in behind her, she's already on the dance floor. They're dangerous, those little pills.

Brussels is another good show, 2-0 so far and, to celebrate, members of the band are to be found at 7 am, knocking up a chemist and demanding he hand over the bicarbonate of soda. One of the poor loves must have had a stomach ache.

The promoters of the German leg are called ASS. Should have taken that for a sign because it's four days of total cack. Miserable audiences, miserable band, miserable crew, miserable weather. A whole day driving in the pissing rain, through never-ending roadworks in the re-unified east. The freedom road? My arse. Just an autobahn for cheap labour. Berlin has changed so much. It's tense, the spirit has disappeared. No one seems happier, neither the westerners nor the easterners. It's going to take some time. It's taken us enough time to get here, due to the traffic, and the gig is almost cancelled. But the lateness is beyond anyone's control this time and a sterling effort is performed by the crew (stand up for the Muzz. Stand up for Jason, Paul Ricketts, Martin Stacey and the Oz man) to get the show on. They needn't have bothered for all this audience is gonna give. A right surly 'impress-me' bunch of mothers. We're wasting our time here, boys.

The only relief comes in Hamburg. Well, it would do with the Reeperbahn, wouldn't it? With a pair of mad eyes I sit in a bar and watch half a dozen transvestites slug it out for a reason I can't make out, ripping each other's clothes off and rolling around the floor. Quite sexy, as it happens, and all for free.

Though we've got a journey of over 300 miles, there's much relief in the crew van when we set off overnight for Switzerland and the beautiful capital city of Berne. There's a joyous outbreak of whistling. The tune is, apparently, from the film *The Great Escape*.

It's time for another loony. We give you Berne's finest. But first we've got to make it up to his house, which is on the side of a mountain. But so's the gig, so we take the funicular railway. Germanic days of darkness are soon forgotten and everyone's back on form. It's like that with touring: one day you're up and the next day you're still up.

The gig is a stormer: it's only a small place, but the mountain people go cra-zee.

'You come in for a post-show drink. Just down the hill there.'
Not many manage to find their way, but Hugo, Simon and the Duff have, and do not regret the effort. I join them for tonight's cabaret. The place is owned by a grizzly bear of a man, the perfect host at first, along with his girlfriend. It is absolutely amazing. A pad

straight out of a seventies' Bond. Gigantic bean-bags and hanging chairs, spiral staircases and sunken floors, split levels and balconies of glistening chrome, sumptuous white shagpiles, on which lie a bevy of purring blondes. All right, it's not that perfect. Most are feline. Not all though, mate, not all. It's snowing outside and settling on the glass roof. There's a veritable blizzard inside and I think we're in danger of being snowed under. Oh, go on then.

We're treated to an endless stream of extreme sports videos and it soon becomes clear our host is in all of them. As the evening wears on he gets more and more hyper, shouting the odds and diving about. One minute he's spinning like a maniac in a hanging chair, the next he's growling and on the hunt for an arm-wrestling opponent – leave off, he'd break your fucking arm. It's a relief when he disappears upstairs, and everybody settles down. I think he's gone to bed … Aaarrgghh-agh-aaarrrggggghhhhh! Oh no, it's fucking Tarzan. There's panic at ground level as he flies off the top floor and comes hurtling down towards us. People scatter as he disappears upwards again. Can you believe it? This bloke is bungy-jumping in his own house. The geezer's a lunatic. Come on, boys. Let's get out of here while he's still tied up. Turns out the place used to be a German bomb factory during the war. That figures.

How on earth do we find these people? How come they keep finding us? I'm glad that that Charlie Manson is still away. He'd be on the tour, wouldn't he?

Paris. Should be good. After all, it's Paris. Girlfriends are on their way, there's an after-show party and it's the last gig of the European leg. No, sometimes things don't always work out as expected. The gig is so-so. It doesn't set the world alight. The ligger contingent has got out of hand and various uninvited dealers are facing off, squabbling over control. It's getting nasty. Backstage it's very tense, boyfriends and girlfriends are arguing, smiles are thin on the ground. An arsehole from the venue, the Elysée Montmartre, starts messing with the T-shirt stand. He's totally out of order, pulling it about and cussing like a good 'un. It all ends up going off, spilling on to the pavement outside, and when others get involved it's nice to see our lot move in for support. When the going got going, crew chief Murray and Jason guitars were there. Family. Still got a cracked cheekbone in the process, though. The after-show at the Roxy seems doomed from the off. It's even worse than expected. Debts are being called in. The vibe is nil. I stay about ten minutes.

Homewards. Not before the van breaks down. And it's still raining buckets.

A break does everyone the world of good, so it's a born-again rabble that boards the plane for Belfast the next weekend. Our local transport is in a minibus that has come up from Dublin and as a result we get pulled at every roadblock and the driver gets grief. A couple of us have to speak up when he's getting the third degree, spoken to in a manner that is totally uncalled for, and nothing short of racist. Funny how the attitude changes when they hear other Brits. All of a sudden they wanna be mates. Guest list is full, pal. Drive on.

The show at the Ulster Hall signals a 100 per cent return to form. It kicked big time. The crowd are as mad as Glasgow, if not madder. Weatherall plays one of his occasional sets of total perfection and the night is suitably rounded off by local boy Glen Molloy. The punters will not leave. The lights go up and they're still having it. The decks are switched off and they're *still* having it. Looks like it's going to be a long weekend.

Masses occupy the Europa Hotel, famous for its claim to be the most bombed hotel in Europe, though I would think the Holiday Inn, Sarajevo may now stake that claim. Belfast's premier club crew, the Sugar Shack crowd, are in and we do our very best to drink the hotel bar dry. I think we succeeded. There were only a couple of bottles of stout left when I staggered out.

There's no room in the van so I attempt to train it to Dublin with the new tour manager, Adey. There's problems on the line so we end up getting a cab. As we approach the 'border' I take a couple of innocuous shots, blot-on-the-landscape kind of stuff, but we're being watched, as is every car that approaches. We're told to leave the road and directed into a huge corrugated shed. We're searched, so is the car. The driver's papers aren't quite in order so that doesn't help. I'm told to hand over the film. I refuse. I've been in much more compromising situations than this and held on to my film, so I'm not about to hand it over to an eighteen-year-old Geordie. A superior is called. He's not much older but is obviously 'officer class'. Fucking chinless wonder and a plum in the mouth. And a right plum he is too. I start to feel sorry for the Geordie, having to serve under this tosser. I'm told the film will be tested, processed, checked and returned if it's 'clean'. Some chance. I know I'll never see it again if I hand it over and it becomes a matter of principle and a battle of wills. They've got nothing to worry about, no 'security has been breached' and it's just a mixture of paranoia and power games. I'm not having it. The squaddie, meanwhile, has unearthed a tour itinerary.

'Primal Scream? Fookin' brilliant, kidda.' Even Lord Snooty is impressed.

We're duly sent on our way. Up the Scream! Ha ha ha ha ha.

How about a crack across the pond? Go west, young man. Go west. First port of call is Philadelphia, home of the Liberty Bell and the seventies' Sound Of. I've got another pal, Pete, on board to do the shirts. I've got to get back midway through the tour as I've started up a dance label with another mate, as well as co-managing his band New Class A. It'll also give me freedom for shooting pics. As Pete hadn't been to the US before, nor for that fact out on the road either, I thought a bit of advice to take it easy wouldn't go amiss. Have the odd night here and there, but remember to do what you've got to do. He certainly went west all right.

It's the first time in the States for Primal Scream also, though they'd been previously for promotion (and Bobby had done it with the Mary Chain), and no one quite knows what to expect. Notoriously conservative in its tastes, the United States had been stuck in a rut of leather pants, high hair and geetar solos for years. I should know, I've still got the cut-offs and headband to prove it.

I had been to some raves on the west coast whilst working for Creation, given the low down by our man in LA, Las Borsai, and, while they were nice-enough happy happy affairs, the party people were predominantly white, middle-class and, I'd say, fairly affluent. The parties certainly didn't have the liberating, egalitarian energy of the do's back home. More like just another fashion rather than the way of life it had become for the legions of Blighty nut-nuts. However, one lasting memory that will remain with me for ever was seeing Mr LSD himself, Dr Timothy Leary, having it large on the dancefloor in a warehouse in downtown LA. What was he? Late sixties? Seventy even? Saucers for eyes and giving the young 'uns a run for their money. Good on ya. Rest in space.

The first gig at the Trocadero is understandably a little edgy but response is good, if not a little bemused. Sceptic tanks seem to like it all right, they just don't know what to do with it. Vitamin deficiency they've got, that's what I reckon it is. The one that comes after D.

Most of the gigs continue in the same light. Good enough, but falling far short of the barminess of Britain. That's to be expected, I suppose, but I wonder if the States will ever wake up. Maybe the races are too polarized for there to be a true acid-house experience, but time will tell.

It's at the gig in New York where I take what kind of becomes the definitive Primal Scream shot, later used both on the 'Rocks' cover and on the inner gatefold of the *Give Out But Don't Give Up* album. Just offstage after an exhaustive performance at the Ritz they simply fell together in the dressing room and I pressed the shutter release. No more complicated than that. It's still one of my favourites. Coming back from my mum's one night, stopping at the lights under the Beckton flyover (right where I used to play as a kid), looking up and seeing that picture, huge all over the walls. Chuffed.

It's pleasing that people I respect rate that shot as well. One such person was B.P. Fallon, legend of the Dublin scene, publicist extraordinaire, and himself the author of an intimate study of U2, having toured the world with them as DJ and vibes man. He came backstage to say hello to the Scream at Dublin stadium on the 'Give Out' tour. He told me he loved this picture and in conversations since has been very supportive and helpful. But I have a confession to make. I couldn't bring myself to say it when I met him for fear of a blanking. He'd be entitled to, as well. He's such a lovely guy and at the risk of him never speaking to me again I can't hide the fact any longer. I feel too bad about it. Remember that night in the Music Machine in Camden? Jam gig. About '78. You were attacked and taken to hospital. It was me. I'm gutted about it. Admittedly both you and I were well pissed at the time and having some kind of heated debate, but I shouldn't have lashed out. I was a right hooligan and can only say I'm very sorry. You're a top bloke.

There's a picture taken in Toronto that almost becomes more famous. Or infamous. And I'm a lot less chuffed about it. As Throb and Denise come into the gig at the RPM I take a quick picture by the ticket booth, in front of a painted wall. There's also a sign that reads 'All exits are final'. I'm horrified when Toby's girlfriend, Liz, comes flying in just after the band have come offstage, screaming for an ambulance. Throb's collapsed and someone is giving him the kiss of life. He's gone a horrible colour and is barely clinging on. I put my hands together and pray I haven't cursed the bloke. Luckily, he's brought to, much to the relief of everyone. There's a tangible state of shock throughout the camp. Worried faces all around. Except for the Throb. He's still up for going out.

Throb has actually been on a full mad one in recent days so this business doesn't come as that much of a surprise. It's a wonder it isn't a more regular occurence to be honest, but on this tour Robert the Throb has been issued a chaperone of sorts, the Scouse about town Steve Shultz ('all right boss'), who is soon better known as Lily. Savage. They're a right win double these two (win double trouble) so instead of one, now you've got two on the missing list. It's thought it might be a good idea to get a chaperone for the chaperone. Adey has totally lost control by this point and money is changing hands on whether he'll last the distance. Get hold of the reins, man, before you crack up.

Highlight of the tour had to be the visit to Hitsville, USA, the home of Tamla Motown. It is like someone's house, too, with a studio out the back. Big clumpy old mixing desk. Knobs the size of teacups. Big old valve amps. Looks so primitive compared to the hi-tech studios of today, but for all the money in the world you couldn't

better what came out of here. Though Motown records have since relocated to LA *this* is the place that turned out some of the greatest music ever made. Songs to make your heart dance: the Supremes, Temptations, the Four Tops. Marvin, Stevie, Smokey. It's enough to make you kneel down and kiss the carpet. Old mods like me and Innes are nearly in tears. We even bump into Berry Gordy's son who had a hit in the eighties under the name of Rockwell. Spawned from the great man. You just want to hug him.

Back at the St Andrew's Hall there's a Scream tribute rendition of 'Ramblin' Rose' in honour of another of Detroit's great musical institutions, Wayne Kramer of the MC5. And with a trip I make to Music Master Records, responsible for numerous house classics and now at the forefront of Detroit techno, visiting this city is like taking a musical heritage tour.

I bow out in Chicago to return to work on the label I've set up with my oldest mate, one Andrew Swallow. He's had quite a name for himself from the football days but was instrumental in the acid-house scene in the East End. If you'd have told me a year before what was about to happen I'd have said you'd have needed locking up. It took Andy more than a few attempts to get me 'out' when it did come along. I never thought it could happen. Going out in the area I grew up in and there not being rows all night. I must have stopped socializing in the east around 1982 - too many glassings and the sweet smell of ammonia. But boy did things change in '88. I'm not saying that angels appeared overnight, but some of the best parties I went to in that time were populated by some of the biggest nutters I've ever known, and a good time was had by all, a serious good time. But that *is* another story.

Andy had also given me the squeeze for my brief but illustrious career in radio. The G-man, Centre Force Radio, 88.3. Keep it locked and London did. Wherever you went you'd hear it. The sound of that summer of '89. Clapham Common on a Sunday. People turning up from raves all over. Lying on the grass with the system on and the sunshine up full, big fat one on the go. Bliss in the sun with your best pals. Let's go London.

I'm happy to return the favour when Andy comes knocking and asks for help on his new project, and find myself back in the world of mailing lists and white labels. Not for that long, as it turned out, due to our money going down when a distribution company put in a phantom order and we end up sitting in an office swamped with overstock, money tied up and unable to get the next release out. Silly me. I forgot how full of shit the music business can be. How it's populated by spineless muppets. The good people really are few and far between. The man responsible in this instance doesn't have any idea of how lucky he is. Call off the dogs. But what goes around comes around and one day for sure, he'll get his.

Back in Chicago I've left Pete Moore in charge of the merchandise with distinct instructions to keep in radio contact. If we needed more stock I had to do it from London. I never heard from the bloke. Another for the missing list. Tales filter back of boxes of shirts left on the streets of Tijuana and Pete riding round in open-top cars. He's gone. Norwich to Hollywood and do not pass go. It happens. The landing is always bumpy, though. It's four hours before his girlfriend Gina finds him akip in a completely different Heathrow terminal from the one he'd arrived in, and gives it to him big-time. Fully justified, too. The rumour that a calling card was found upon his person with the legend 'You've Been Screamed' is still unsubstantiated.

I take back the reins for the mini-tour that is built around the first

Brixton Academy show the band did in March '92. It would become like the annual works day out. Book a week off, it's the Scream at Brixton. Portsmouth and Birmingham gigs thrown in for good measure and call the lot 'Shot to Pieces'. STP. Give yourself a blood change. You might need it after all this. But a terrible toothache in Portsmouth. Birth of an abcess. Agony and I can't bear it. But how I got looked after! Every two minutes there's a knock at my door and it's another deranged Dr Feelgood with another new plan. Just a little bit of this and a little bit of that – that should do it. It'll make you feel better, boy. So considerate, these people.

It's a roadblock. Brixton to the river. Tickets are top dollar outside the tube. Well, what do you reckon? Primal Scream at midnight. Weatherall, Oakenfold, Paterson, Norman Jay, Mark Moore. Three rooms of music. 6 am curfew? Yes, please. This *is* the rock 'n' roll circus. The blueprint many have since followed but none have bettered. Legendary. 'Don't fight it, feel it'. Go on, D. Ain't a band in the world that can touch them tonight.

It's also the night of the ketamine Es. London was swamped with them at the time and unscrupulous dealers have flooded the hall. To say people were bouncing off the walls would be the understatement of the year. People who use their limbs like that are usually in a circus. I've never seen anything like it. Yes I have, that cinema scene in *Gremlins*. Hi ho. Hi ho. Ho ho. Ho Ho. Oi ho. Oi oi. Oi Oi!

Girlfriend Karen and I have taken off for Cuba, just in time for the Mayday parade. LA burns as I watch Fidel receive a million blessings on the streets of Havana. The irony is not lost. Forget parading the guns and the tanks, get the bikes out and pass the rum, and dance all night in the name of the revolution. I didn't see any of these people waving with a gun forced to their heads. It's tough there, that's for sure, but for that you have to thank old Uncle Sam. Still smarting because they took the ball away. While I was there the US forced Mexico to stop a boat full of humanitarian aid and medical supplies docking in the port. Threatened trade suspension to increase the suffering. You lovely people.

Glastonbury. From strength to strength. Ask anyone who was there. The night of the century. The Orb as the sun went down, followed by the Scream. A sea of arms. Mental and wicked and wild. It's one of those emotional nights that'll last for ever. The walk back to the dressing room cabin is a march of victory. Everyone so happy. Time to celebrate, break out the champers. Oh dear, Sheertaft's got there first and has made off with the rider. Chin-chin. Congratulations. Have a nice cup of water. The bus is laden, have no fear, and guests come and go throughout the night and electronic tags might be a good idea as a quick little wander could be a wander too far. The glory of sunrise up on the Green Field, the tent with Harry Hare's Krishna technopop, the brandy coffees when there's a nip in the air, the loons in madmax-a-mobiles creeping past me and Bob tipping their crushed top hats with a wink and a 'Morning!'. It's a madhouse out there and the best little madhouse in the whole of the world. Denmark whoop the Germans in the final of the Euro championship, too. Oh, sweet revenge.

I don't know what happened but I wake up sweating and crawl out of the bunk in the need of some air and maybe another brandy coffee. Step out on to the Somerset lawn to face a … runway. What??!! There's a fucking jumbo heading right my way and as I run for cover I swear I'll kill that bloke with the blotters. But it really is a runway that the bus is parked up against. Admittedly there's a fence in between but I've never been this close before. Then I realize I must have been kidnapped. What for? Half a dozen STP shirts? I know everyone wanted one but this is a joke. A face appears and it's

a face I know. The bus driver. He's bloody in on it. Points into the distance.

'You look like you need a wash.' All right mate, no need to get personal. 'There's the hotel.' What? I'm not being funny mate, but where am I? 'Gatwick. Your plane leaves in an hour.' Go on, tell me, Beirut is it, by any chance, you fucking kidnapping bastards? He shakes his head with a look that says not you as well and disappears back into his cab.

Actually it's Copenhagen. Wonderful. Wonderful. Not the Danish Liberation Army either. It's that Nightingale. I completely forgot or couldn't remember. He'd booked another gig after the 'bury. Roskilde away. What's he doing to us? How we all make it to check-in is nothing short of a miracle, yet a few hours later they're up there again, rocking the Danes 'til the cows come home. It's 3 am and we're leaping about as Weatherall consolidates the damage. Gat Decor. Passion? *Fucking stop it, I tell ya!*

Told ya. Knew someone would get hurt. Just happens to be me. The back has gone. I mean gone. I mean not even Granddad with a stick gone. I mean will I ever walk again gone. Evil. Pain. Pain. Pain. On the floor the day we get back. That'll teach me. I'll be in a wheelchair for the rest of my life. But what a weekend.

Hospitals, osteopaths, specialists, traction. Therapy, painkillers, tears and the blues. End of the T-shirts. No more boxes or lifting like that. No more jogging and you're just a young man. No more playing football - *what!* Give me a lethal one now, doc, you can't do that to me, you can't do that. Give me my boots back, I'm gonna play for England one day.

The band complete a fine summer with more headliners at the Féile in Ireland and the Hultsfred Festival in Sweden, where I understand there's a hotel fracas involving some uppity young Mancs. Oasis or something I think they were called.

So everything's going very, very well. Album of the year and the Mercury award. First one at that. A right do at the Savoy. Moet for days. It's not Bob's scene, though, and he lasts barely a minute. Hijacked the limo and off to Tim Tooher's. What a motley crew go to collect the prize. Alex Nightingale shouting his head off, Duffy in circles, Innes and the Throb in Mott-the-Hoople coats, Denise looking a million dollars, Toby, Hugo and H all whistled up, Arden doing a tune on the bugle, Simon Stevens looning about. What must people think? It's like a day trip from Broadmoor. Acceptance speech courtesy of the Archbishop (one of the family) that has the whole place in stitches. What it's got to do with the band nobody knows. Compere for the night Richard Jobson sidles up to Toby and asks under his breath, 'Who's that? Where the fuck is Bobby Gillespie?'
'Oh, don't worry pal, he's just popped round his mate's to play some records.'
Within the hour they've lost the award and they've lost the cheque. That's gratitude for you.

What's more important for all concerned is the miners' benefit gig up at Sheffield Arena with the Orb, Oakey, Justin Robertson and Lewis Gough.

Biggest show in England so far and it's time to give a bit back. Even a twisted idiot would have to admit that the miners on this island have had a pretty rough deal. Communities destroyed by that maniac blue-rinse. All part of the plan. It changed this country for ever, and don't tell me for the better. First the miners. Then the print. Even the nurses. The *nurses* , for God's sake.

Bob Gillespie Senior knows what's what, been working his nuts off for the children of Chernobyl, so it's no great surprise that the Scream are doing this gig. But no song and dance for some media points, just do the show, get hold of the cash and pass it on. It won't get their jobs back but it'll put food on the table. Good work people.

What a way to end the year. I think Nightingale is getting it right. Australia. It's summer while it's winter in the UK, so pack your shorts! Only a week but a week will do. One show in Melbourne. One in steak and kidney, right on the beach. Not that you can stay in the sun too long. Twenty minutes walk in the centre of Melbourne and I end up with the top of my earholes roasted well done. Unheard of.

The Aussies have already had the conversion and are well up for it. Party party crowd, good shows, good times. Times that remind you how lucky you are, I won't deny it. Keeping fit, too. Back exercises in the morning and jaw exercises all night. Six of us squeeze in a car after Sydney and head south 100 km to an outdoor rave. Happy Valley is actually on the top of a cliff looking over the gorgeous Shell Harbour and I'm in my element amongst the elements. We're away!

Trouble is getting back. Candles have been burnt at both ends as well as the sides. Ten-minute shifts is the best anyone can do at the wheel and it takes us forever to make it back. We were the lucky ones: we learn of a pile-up that explained the traffic and major diversion. Fatalities have been high and rave hysteria breaks out in the press.

We move on to Japan. More of the same. What is it about the place? Everyone goes mental. This time it's the Innes. Attacks Throb, Oz and Jacko (the Manchester sound patrol) with a fire extinguisher. He has his reasons, so he says. I'm in my room some time later and it's all off again outside. Now it's the Throb's turn, who's done Innes's door with an almighty kick and catches him on the phone, defences down. Naked. Within seconds he's lost in a thick white cloud as a CO_2 special is emptied out. The fire bells are ringing and hotel staff appear in gas masks with torches ready to evacuate the guests. Innes is thankfully decent by this time and it's nice to see him back in men's clothing. When the dust settles (literally) it's nothing short of post-nuclear. The hotel is called the Osaka Grand. Oh dear, it'll cost a few. I don't know what's the matter with these boys, behaving like that in a hotel. They want to grow up.

It was also a mistake to leave that huge $40,000 cake sculpture down in the lobby. Alex Nightingale got the munchies after a proper post-gig '88 set in a local club courtesy of the good doctor Paterson. Ate a good $500-worth before security saw him off. That's the band's manager now, by the way.

In an echo of the previous year the final gig is an all-nighter at Club Citta, Kawasaki and it's just as mad. Dancing all night 'til they close it down. Al McGee's in town and is buzzed, having just met Jacko. Not the onstage soundman Jacko, but that other bloke with the funny hat. Bit of a mover I have to agree, but can't sing half as good as our Jacko. Bob and Throb are now busking out on the street with an acoustic guitar, entertaining the fans with a medley of songs. A perfect post-party chill-out scene, except they happen to be outside Kawasaki station with rush hour approaching. Commuters try to

avoid eye contact but it's hard when you've got Simon Stevens haranguing you with an upturned cap. Collection for the people. Beer and fags. That's a great thing about Japan. Vending machines all over the place. Cigarettes, hot coffee, crisps, nuts (oh no), beer, edible panties (what?). Can you imagine that back in Britain, a machine selling beer? Wouldn't last two minutes, would it? Especially when, at 2 am, an internal last bell closes the thing down. You can picture the scene now, 'You what? Refuse my custom?' as they kick the machine all the way down the high street. What's the matter with us? No really, why are we so different? You see it all over. People lobbing gear out of cars. Attitude. Shitting on the doorstep. No respect except for self. You might think it's rich when you consider earlier tales but let's make a start. It's not that difficult, is it? Put it in the fucking bin, litter lout.

Excuse me for a minute while I climb down from this high horse here and on we'll go. It's a very hard task for Dai and Shin, our boys from Smash, who try their best to round us all up to get us to the airport in time for our flight. We're late, and now it's the rush hour. We get stuck in traffic and Nightingale is like a madman, out the van and weaving between lorries, telling them to get a move on. He's clucking like a mad mother hen. Stevens is all over the place, tears and all, and I think there's been a bit of a falling out. Hugo's not speaking at all and there's some concern. The police arrive, throw open the door and demand to know what's going on. Before Schultz can grab him, Duffy is up, totally slaughtered, with a 'D'ya know how the Villa got on, mate?'. That threw 'em. There's a pool of goodies and a veritable pick 'n' mix it is, too. Mmm, may as well have a bit of a walnut then.

Now why didn't I listen to Pete Townshend? I've seen that documentary loads of times, too. Him recounting the horrors of taking acid on a plane, which as a result put him off the cardboard bits for life. Well I can't say it was that bad, but it was a confusing eleven hours, that's for sure. Luckily, me, Innes and a couple of others have been upgraded to business, with double-wide seats and personal videos. Normally, for a flight of this duration, this would be a right touch, but I may just as well have been strapped in the dentist's. Didn't leave the seat once. Transfixed and puzzled by that little screen. Didn't think to turn it off. Even when it came on top. Able to choose from several films I did so, constantly. Two minutes would be enough before I'd start to freak out and skip the channels for a kinder vibe. This was pointless, because even that Bugs Bunny bloke you can't trust. I know he's plotting some evil deed. I know it, I can see it in his eyes. See those teeth, he'd chop your head off soon as look at you man. The blood'll be gushing all over the place and what's left of your body will start drowning in it and then he'd get that carrot, insert a couple of razors and … *Aarrgggh! Get it off!* See what I mean, and that was only about one minute thirty.

When I look across the aisle and see the way my spar is gripping the armrests, I'm happy to know I'm not alone. In fact, by the look of him I'm having it easy. There's never a question of doing a mad one and heading for the exit door kind of nonsense – I'm far too busy changing channels. See that Mary Poppins? You can't trust her, you know. That spoonful-of-sugar business is all a front. Spoonful-of-poison more like. Assassin. That's what she is.

I wonder how they're getting on back in economy.

Back just in time for Christmas to be spent at my girlfriend Karen's mum's, we fly up to Glasgow. I arrive and fall on the bed before my bags hit the floor and sleep for the best part of a week.

Left Hugo Nicholson. Glastonbury.
Right Boston.

Above Sydney. Australia. **Below** 'Is that 504?' Melbourne.
Right Clonmel. Ireland.

S.F.X. Dublin.

Left Miners Benefit. Sheffield Arena.
Above Brixton Academy. London. **Below** The guest list.

Above Scream Heights before the milkman's been. EC1. London.
Below T-shirts at the Ritz. New York.

The Archbishop. Sheffield Arena.

Mama's Pearl. Denise Johnson. Motown. Detroit.

Above 'And if you're young at heart, rise up and take your stand'. Motown. Detroit.
Below Justin Robertson, Em Hughes and the Throb. Sheffield Arena.

Above Exeter.
Below Arriving. Glastonbury.

Above Sydney.
Below Bunka Hall. Yokohama. Japan.

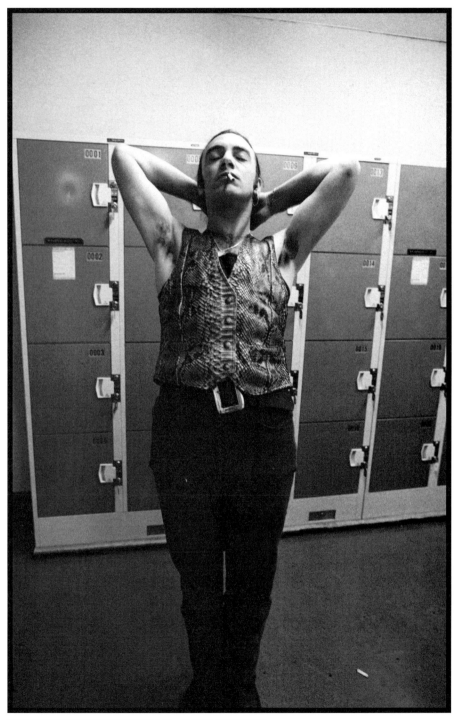

Left 6a.m. I staggered out of the Throb's room, the lift doors opened and … Japanese fans. Nikko Hotel. Kawasaki.
Right Yokohama. Japan.

Left Picking up tips just before we leave for Glastonbury. Exeter.
Right I don't believe you. On the road. UK.

Left Bob about to go onstage. First US gig. Trocadero. Philadelphia.
Above Alex Paterson and the Throb. Chicago. **Below** Down the Metro, planning the next move.

Above Bobs away. Mercury Music Awards. Savoy Hotel. London.
Below *Screamadelica* wins.

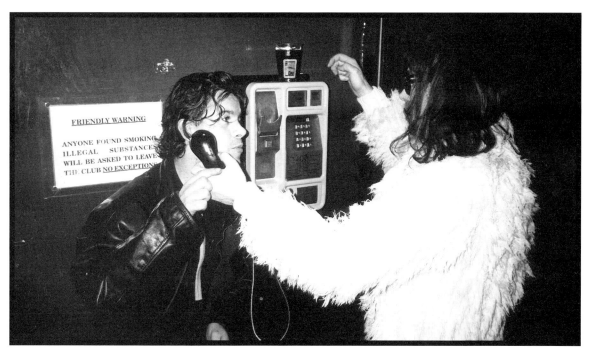

Above The last person seen with the award. The Savoy.
Below Innes and Duff calling the Savoy to check if they know who was the last person seen with the award. After-party at The Milk Bar.

Chicago.

Toronto.

1993

What a year. One I wouldn't want to see repeated. It all started out fine as well, but I suppose it goes like that. Finally get the back problem explained, and, as the T-shirt thing is over, it's time to get off travelling again, cameras an' all, and see what's to be found. Besides, the Scream are fairly inactive. They're not meant to be – in fact, they're ensconced in a studio in Chalk Farm getting the next album together, except it isn't quite turning out that way. It's not a very productive time. A foe has entered the camp and is in danger of taking over. Disarray reigns. The sum total of this winter of discontent? Zero. Half a chorus and a Kit-Kat bar. Someone had better get a grip, and fast.

After a horrific bout of salmonella poisoning at home in London I decide it's safer abroad. I head East for a referendum in Russia and further East again to cover elections in Cambodia, with every intention of joining up with the others when they decamp to Memphis later that spring. Cambodia is an experience too far. All I'd expected and a little bit more. The Khmer Rouge on the run. Mine patrol with the French Foreign Legion. Swooping in on Chinooks over Angkor Wat with lunatic Russian 'topguns' at the helm. The pride and joy at the polling stations. The hospitality and warmth of a people with a history so horrific you and I can't even imagine in our worst nightmares. Everybody lost somebody.

I hang out in Laos in a Golden Triangle haze and await directions about Tennessee. I'm very pissed off when, despite umpteen faxes and playing a waiting game, I do not receive any info from Scream Heights HQ. Very slack. As a result you won't see pictures from those Memphis sessions and if any do exist they won't be from me. What a waste. Still, there were much worse things facing me when I returned home in the height of summer, so looking forward to so many things. You could have knocked me down with a feather. 'Cept it felt like a ten-ton truck. My girlfriend is leaving. Then she isn't. My stepfather, Ray, is seriously ill. We're getting married. Then we're not. Then we are. Ray died, and the world is poorer. (May he rest in peace.) And now we're not getting married. Again. So it's goodbye then, goodbye to a part of me.

These are the times when you find out who your true friends are. Martin Stacey, I love you, you saved my life. Kept me fed when I couldn't face food. There to listen, and listen, and listen. Big sis Bren, Mr Cracknell too. Nina, Cat and Lisa B, Rob and D. I must have driven them mad. They said it'll take time and sure it did. What else was it, Marty? 'What doesn't kill you makes you stronger.' That's right, mate.

Sabresonic. Happy Jax. London Bridge. It helped a lot and got me out. Before you know it, I'm an ever-present. Even on my own, I didn't care. It was that kind of club, and I could walk home. Hearing 'Smokebelch' was a complete revelation. Rebirth of love, if only for music. Weatherall on scintillating form. Those dynamite ciders. The floor tipped up. The Scream would appear. McGee's about. All the faces not since Pure, not since Shoom. That kind of club. Tunes! Leftfield and Lydon, Weller and Lynch. Open Up. The Cosmos. Year Zero.

Fireworks night. Off to Clapham to meet Alex and Bob G – Jerry Lee Lewis at the Grand. On my way out of the flat, the lift doors open and I almost fall over. It's my neighbour. She issues a blank while her mum does the talking. Never set eyes on her before, but at this moment I can't keep them off. Fireworks night. You could say that again. Chased her down. Notes on the car and schoolboy capers. Things can only get better.

One night after Sabresonic we're all round McGee's. He and I used to share a flat but now he lives in the next block along. Bobby and Alex fight like kids over CDs. Me next! No, me next! So on and so on. It's 8 am and I say, 'I'll call my neighbour!'

'You can't do that Granty, wake people up at this time of the morning'.

Want a bet? Twenty-four hours later we tumble out of the Ministry of Sound and a brand new friendship has begun. Jenny Mitchell. Enthused me and inspired me, a burst of sunshine. If I tumble into another relapse, you just keep on banging and won't let me hide. Dragged me out when it all got too much. Shook me down and perked me up. You'd had a rough time, too, but didn't let on. And it's you that night, again round McGee's, who's off in the morning to meet the Scream in LA, who gets behind me when I say I fancy going as well. It's the kick up the arse I sorely need. Get out there and get working again. It was the best thing I could ever have done. Thank you, girl.

What a dilemma. Flight goes early on Saturday but how can I miss Sabresonic? Simple. Pack first and get up the road. Sweat till the end. Straight to the airport. You'll believe a man can fly. A last cheeky half before customs LA. Straight to the Ocean Wave Studio. Hello, boys! We're out tonight. By midnight I'm climbing up a tree. By 3 am it's all a blur. Speeding along highways in downtown LA, weaving our way through gilded towers. Might as well be on Mars. 6 am, I split from the pack. Gotta keep going. Frustration explodes. Psychedelia rave in a dubious town. 9 am, I'm back on the bus. (Forget about us. Put the blame on me.) Who looks madder, me or my fellow passengers? Without a doubt they got the vote. Heading for Hollywood with a Hollywood head. Sixty hours up and I need to crash. I know those faces jumping out of the cab. The Throb, Duff and Alex going shopping. 10 am, a couple of bottles of 'Gentleman Jack'. I know you. Any chance of a lift?

Come Monday I'm horizontal. After months of hibernation I admit I've just been on the bender of a lifetime. Absolutely caned it big time. It just had to be done. I got a lot out of my system and put a lot in. Now I am paying the price. Eyes, ears nose and throat, every bone from head to toe done in. It never seems such a good idea does it, the morning after the three days before?

Several days are spent in Ocean Wave Studio on Sunset Boulevard, but at the scruffy end near where the buses turn and you can find proper burritos. The band record a track for the new album. 'Call On Me', overseen by producer George Drakoulias, is a rousing big Faces-style rocker of a song. Spirits are high and I feel like I'm alive again.

It was on this trip I really hit it off with the Throb. We hadn't been that close over the years, and I'd never thought we had that much in common. But on my arrival he's the first to offer lodgings. The band have got two-room suites in Le Parc and the put-you-up's mine if I want it. Done. Well, Robert Young, I'm pleased to meet ya, a more generous and genuine bloke you couldn't hope to meet. Maniac, of course, as well, but a generous and genuine maniac at that.

As the week goes on the room rarely sees light, the curtains remain drawn and room-service trays pile up. Every bin is full, every bottle is empty. Throb's not into a visit by room service, and normally I'd agree – why make people's jobs any harder? Who needs your bed made every day? I hate being fussed over. I'm sure the Guatemalan room-maid would rather be at home with her kids anyway, but mid-week I have to have a purge. There are things growing under the sofa and we're two potatoes away from having the room condemned. I try to get the rubbish out of the door but it's hard when the band's manager is wedged up against it, 100 per cent comatose.

Throb swears I'm on the phone for a good half an hour gabbing away, then start having an almighty row, which ends with me slamming it down. 'Who was that G?'

'Fucking answer machine, Throb, fucking answer machine.'

I'm in love again ah-ahhhhh. The Buzzcocks at the Viper Room and me and Bob are inches away from having a pogo. Go on, you start. No, go on, you start.

Remember at the circus when they put the bloke in the cannon? Light the fuse and off he goes? That's me on the crystal (crystal methedrine - purest amphetamine). Superman in a Sabrettes shirt. Running up Santa Monica Boulevard and not stopping for lights. It's only fifty-five miles per hour limit here, too. I'll lose my licence.

Is it any surprise I collapse when I get back to London? Two weeks in bed with a serious flu. Well I've certainly got no one else to blame. My neighbour Jenny's soups just keep on getting better. 'Gold Blend', Throb calls her.

Christmas Eve and it's me and Jenny, Alex and Alan Magoo. No great plans, but a we're on a mission. Give us an M. *M!* Give us a D. *D!* Give us an M. *M!* Give us an A. *A!* What have you got? Double vision and a crashed car before we've even left the offices in EC1. We end up at RAW in the YMCA where there's a realization that this is no ordinary gear. It's rocket fuel and we've lost all contact with Mission Control. I'm well and truly off the radar but my body is having the time of its life. Back in Rotherhithe the journey continues and there are moments when I wonder if anyone's actually got a map 'cos it's a long way back down and there's a serious danger of someone getting lost.

I arrived at my dad's very late for Christmas dinner, but at least I made it. Nightingale was found later that day, fast asleep under a table in RAW, Alan made do with a sandwich of sausage, Jenny crashed out at her mum's. On the way to my dad's I was driving through Docklands and past a deserted Canary Wharf. Big open spaces. European home. Somehow it looked the most beautiful place on earth. 'Move On Up' by Curtis from the speaker comes. What a feeling. So high. I remember laughing out loud. Didn't think I'd make it here, but things change, don't they? No matter how bad things get, they can get better. You've got to keep on telling yourself that. It's hard sometimes but you've got to keep on telling yourself that. And when it *is* better you savour the day and use every second as though it's your last. Happy Christmas.

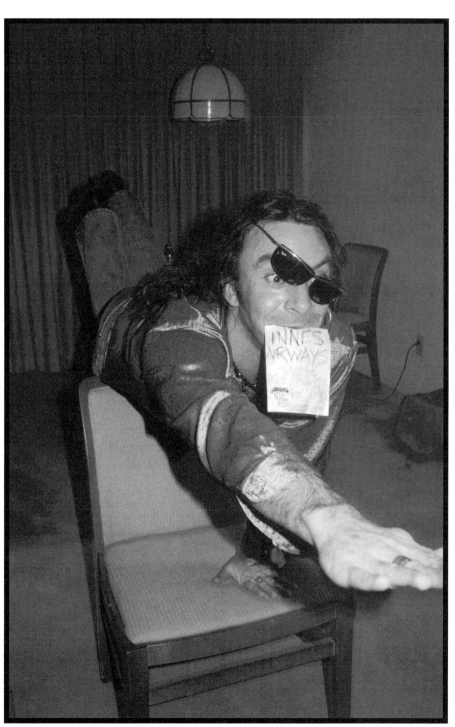

Previous page A gift for el Presidente. Alan McGee. Ocean Wave Studios. Hollywood.
Above Flying high. Le Parc Meridan Hotel. West Hollywood.

Crash Landing.

King of the Joanna that is. Ocean Wave Studios. Hollywood.

*If you're broke down
and you're needing a ride
If you're feelin'
more dead than alive
If you're hungry
and you're needing a feast
If you wanna get drunk
every night of the week ...*

Call on me.

I heard ya.
I'm on the first plane to L.A.

Los Angeles.

1994

This is the year it really goes off. If you can't take the heat keep out of the furnace. Seatbelts on, rocks off, honey. We're back in the basement of the YMCA but Alex is awake now. It's a video shoot in Billion Dollar Babes, one of the clubs of the moment, all big-lips glitter, hot-pants and fur (fake of course, and glorious amounts). It's an excuse for a party, an excuse for a gig. Director Matthew Ames tries to remind everyone 'This is a VIDEO!' as Innes riffs 'Satisfaction' in platform boots. Bobby tight in velvet, Denise divine in lace. Day becomes night, night becomes day. Off to a flying start.

New York, New York, so good and half the price. Jeff Barrett of Heavenly Records and Publicity packs me off on a plane to cover a big, and most anticipated, meet. Primal Scream and George Clinton, together at last. 'Funky Jam' for MTV.

Sabresonic to the airport, transatlantic and out - this is becoming a habit – no bad one at that. Irish bar, Vietnamese food, me and Jeff on the lurch. Lift to a loft, a Factory crowd. Wade through the posing and avoid the pretence. It's *Midnight Cowboy*, '94. I know that lot over there by the decks. Evenin' all, what's the coup?

It's that crystal gear again. Only in America. Junior Vasquez. The Sound Factory. Doesn't get much better than that. It's almost midday by the time I escape and then I'm marching, hood up, eyes out – even crack dealers step back – weaving my way through the streets of sleaze. Just keep on going, crosstown to the other side.

Who's this gang of street punks, all leathered up? YEAH? GET OUT OF MY FUCKING … It's Throb, Bob the G, Duff, Innes, Jeff. Head-down oblivion, not a care where I'm going or where I am, but nonetheless very determined to arrive, I can't believe I've bumped into them. Pure coincidence! At three in the afternoon! It just so happens it's outside our hotel. Bob turns the tables and takes a picture of me – it'll scare small children [See About the Author]. Good job the band were there, or I'd still be marching now.

It's a glorious day at MTV and there's a squabbling queue thrusting autograph books, paying respects at the court of King George Clinton. He can tell a tale or two. Larger than life and living it large. We're beginners in the game. D and George are at the mike together and the ice caps start melting, which we need, as a blizzard descends on NYC and your nose drips to ice. Better keep talking or it's frozen lips. Warnings abound: do not leave your homes unless it's absolutely necessary. People are getting stranded and are told to stay in their cars. One man braves the elements and you have to be in awe. Fearless of frostbite, immune to the cold, risking all to clear a path to the convenience store. It's Innes – he's run out of Guinness.

It's too good here. I'm staying, at least 'til the crystal's done. See ya, boys. Get Jenny out and do the sights. 'Jackie 60' birthday night.

Strip-glam queens and tranny boys. With a plastic skirt, you're a native New Yorker. Full-on 'mob' party with Neville Limelight. Shown the door when he starts showing off. A debauched residence, Hotel Gramercy Park. Shoot 'Tripmaster Monkey' for the record company. 'Vincent's' hot sauce in Little Italy. I can take it. *In the Name of the Father* by the Chelsea Hotel. Vasquez again, this time with my girl. Rocking the dancefloor, rolling under the bar. If you're gonna be outrageous, just once in your life, look no further than the big bad apple. And take the hugest, *hugest* bite.

Back in London there's a dispute over unfinished T-shirt business. Nightingale and I have had our differences over the years, and at Terminal rehearsal studio it's gone off again on the eve of the UK tour. Fuck it, I'm out, stick your tour right where the sun don't shine. Murray the crew boss smoothes the ranks but I still won't have it. Innes rings up later that night: 'Get on the fucking bus, Fleming.'
'Yeah, okay then, just for one gig, just to get some pictures, and then I'm gone, 'cos if I see that fuckin' Nightingale … '
Of course, I'm still there at the end of the tour – where else would I want to be? And I've sorted it with Alex, too. That's the end of all that now, no need for such rubbish, life's too short.

After an opener in Northampton it's north of the border and Ayr Pavilion. Innes and I exchange blank stares. Celtic have lost to Falkirk of all people and the Hammers have gone out to Luton, both in their respective Cup campaigns. Glory gone for another year. Better stick together. It won't be long before the Chelsea and Rangers fans find out. Bastards.

Susan McGee, sister of Alan, has turned up and comes back to the bus for a couple of drinks. I didn't see her go, though, and that's a bit rude, not saying goodbye. Oh well, she must have been a couple of sheets to the wind.

The storm outside makes for a terrible journey across the Irish sea. It's a relief to reach Belfast where one by one people tumble out of the bunks. 'Mornin' D. Bob. Henry. All right Duff? Andrew. Sus … Susan!'
That explains it.
'Where am I?'
Don't know how to tell you this, but you know that other island? No, not Skye …
She's supposed to have opened her shop in Glasgow at ten. Off to the airport, then. That's an expensive little night out.

There's a few new faces amongst the camp.
Steve 'Sid' Sidelnyk on drums, ex-Style Council. An electronic genius and doesn't drink – sure he's read the job description?

Paul Harte – Hartie. He's team coach – good vibes and care, twenty-four carat gem. Old schoolfriend and musical collaborator of Bob and the Throb and Scream member there at the start. He goes back longer than any of us - wonder how he's kept sane? That's easy – he hasn't.

Phil 'Trigger' Hamilton on tour management, ex-PIL and Eraserhead. Bridge House, Canning Town '78, we remember, we remember. Trig has the distinction of being the only Chelsea fan in the whole of East London. Don't know what happened there; his mother must have dropped him on his head when he was a baby.

Kris Needs. Tour DJ, ex-everything, done more than you can shake a stick at. The spiky-haired joker in the pack. Carry on up the Faces. Kris and his partner Wonder are Secret Knowledge, the Ike and Tina of Techno.

Steven Molloy is Fatty. He's on security. MadMan, he's a legend in his own waistline, ex-backline boy for the House of Love. I know all about Fatty. So do the police: he led their climbing team up the Himalayas as a teenager. It's true enough.

'Rocks' had been a big hit and, with the success of the *Give Out, But Don't Give Up* album, this seventeen-date tour is a sell-out. Unlike the *Screamadelica* tour these shows end early, and are played in more traditional venues. The band turn in a stormer, night after night. It's got the dance element but it's well rocked-up, punky groovy party.

We're back in Belfast at the Europa again, and what better way to celebrate than to head straight for breakfast from the all-night bar. Fresh orange, please, and a drop of vodka. Batting on after, in one of the rooms, there's the usual palaver going on, nothing so dramatic – but the looks we got from the window cleaner slowly winching his way past the window! Shouldn't be such a nose ointment.

The Man U and Villa contingent fly back into London for the Coca-Cola Cup final. That's basically half-a-dozen reds against the Duff. Last laugh to the Brummies. The pain is eased a few days later when the show in Manchester just happens to be on the same day as Liverpool at Old Trafford – coincidence, that. 3-0 should cheer 'em up. As usual for Man United home games, supporters come from afar, and the Brittania Hotel bar is awash with lunatic Danes, Irish reds, local drunks and our motley crew. It is totally out of control, like a kindergarten with a barman.

Guest DJ for the night was Brother Marco, he of the Young Disciples, been known to donate a bassline or two in his time as well, to our lot here and Weller the modfather, for starters. He and his brother take refuge in the corner with an eager Bob G and are caning countless pots of tea. Joined now by Needsy, but he's not stupid, he won't get involved with that rubbish. Sticking with a treble JD and coke. Wise man, that. See what tea does to people. That's Marco on the ivories, that is. The whole bar is up, jiving and a-twisting and thirty pissed Danes are doing the conga. It's a disgusting, evil scene of depravity and I vow on the spot to never let myself go so low.

Liverpool at Cream and then Glasgow. Remember Bannockburn? How could I forget, Innes, with the likes of you around? Leeds, we'll have a quiet one, it's a Sunday. Someone forgot to tell Dave Beer, he of the legendary Back to Basics. Have a little private one in his mate's restaurant if we want. Well, you're only young once and it was party of the tour I'd say, with snowball fights and pogoing to the Clash and the Pistols. It's a free-for-all. Sorry I haven't mentioned much about gigs. Suffice to say it's magic every night.

Cambridge. Anybody seen Duffy? He hasn't shown in the dressing room since the band came off. Think he'd had a drink or two, but he'll show up. The last bit of the stage the crew pack down is the drum riser. Who's this? The Duff. Soundo. He must have left the keyboards and crawled straight under it. Nice to know he's safe and warm. Temaze party back at the hotel. Now it's my turn.

Southampton. Too much Guinness. I'm running along the bar. Those boys know how to wind me up. Sling on the Pistols and I'm off. Fatty's got me bearhugged and is red-carding me to bed, but I'm not finished yet. Party in Bob's room. Then to the swimming pool. You can't come in here, sir, without the proper attire. Fatty liberates swimwear from the gym shop for us all: swimsuits, ladies' thongs and gear like that. This is getting out of hand.

Cardiff. EMF boys. Pace it, fellas, you wouldn't be throwing up in the wastebin if you did.

London. Oh, leave me alone. Three nights at Brixton Academy. Three! Prepare the stretchers. But wait a minute. Saturday night, and it's Primal Scream with George Clinton: the Mothership lands in SW9. You won't see many gigs like that in your life. I don't think they told Innes there was a gig the next night. Man was sleeping by his amp.

Brighton (storming show, by the way). Will this ever end? I've got to get to the marbles shop before they shut. Annie Nightingale is leaving her lovely old house. What better send-off than set up the decks, invite everyone round, and party 'til dawn. It's the last day of the tour, so no time to lose – everyone back to the Grand Hotel, occupy a suite and get room service in. Champagne on the balcony, a good day to you all. *Know what I mean?*

I cut out from most of the European tour. I'm heading south, as far as you can go in a straight line. Johannesburg for the first South African democratic elections. It's the most amazing experience in my life and a privilege to be there. Tears of joy. The street party of the century. I don't think I'll take a better picture than I did that night. Goosebumps. To think I met the man, the only hero I want to have. Nelson was thanking me – thanking me! – for the efforts of the British Anti-Apartheid movement. This was it, the moment that made it all worthwhile. We were vindicated for every march, vigil, campaign, for every shout raised in anger. You can make a difference, Nelson Mandela told me so. Long live the President.

In March I moved in with Jenny. In June I had to move out. Maybe it's too early. We need our space. There's a room available above Alex's office in EC1. Scream Heights. And higher. There's a shower, I've got a toaster, what more do I need? All-night cafes and a pub that opens at 4 am due to the close proximity of Smithfield Meat market. A bit too close, as it happens, for someone who doesn't eat meat. This place becomes home for a year and looking back I don't know how. It was essentially a box of an office with a flop out sofa-bed. At least I lived near to my work.

WED 11 MAY – LONDON – SAN FRANCISCO

Suddenly it's Heathrow, the tannoys calling for the last six remaining passengers on BA287 to San Francisco. Throb's still in the duty free. Some things never change.

Today the Scream depart Britain for the best part of three months, on a tour that comprises two months coast-to-coast USA opening for Depeche Mode, with the odd gig of their own thrown in between. A long time, a long way – what will happen between now and then? Only time will tell … As with any long-haul flight the plan is to swallow as much alcohol as possible before the school dinners arrive, drop a valium10 before your first bite, do two wines, chase with a brandy and, bingo, you should pass out before the trays are cleared. This way you should beat the jet-lag, therefore enabling you to go out the minute you land. There's plenty of toi-toi dancing in the aisles in celebration of the previous days historic inauguration of Nelson the man down in free South Africa. We drop in sharp over the bay of San Fran on a gloriously bright sunny day, though Alcatraz island looks ominous – will it be on the itinerary for the odd member somewhere on this tour?

THURS 12 MAY – CAL EXPO – SACRAMENTO – JOHN SMITH, R.I.P

Sad news of the Labour Party leader John Smith's death filters through from London and an air of shock and disbelief descends. There's a stand-off in the Hilton lobby as Throb, Duff and Stevie Molloy stroll (with fags on) right into a no-smoking convention. If looks could kill … fear and loathing and we're still a week from Vegas. Before we are all shot by a crazed nicotine-free health fascist we're shuffled on to the bus for the short ride to Cal Expo. Apparently, most of the venues on this two-month schlep across the States are to be like this. Huge (between 10,000 and 20,000 seats), purpose-built amphitheatres where the 'young' and the 'free' can 'let themselves go' – strict curfew 11 pm. Plenty of hot-dog and Coke stands, tacky merchandise stalls, clean toilets and ample parking but for one raised in the spit-and-speed punkhalls through the dry-ice drugsmosphere of the houses of acid, this strikes me as being just a little bit safe. Tame. Sterile. About as much to do with rock 'n' roll as American football's got to do with football.

Fears are confirmed as the crowd queues patiently and politely and, though desperate to reach the front when the gates open, when the big bad security man (you know he's important, he's got a walkie-talkie!) says 'Don't RUN', they don't run. Filing in in a nice orderly manner to stake a place where their idols the Mode may gaze upon them and where the girls can pretend to wet their pants and the boys can pretend to be girls. It's all so rad(ical), dude. Backstage it's no better, there's round passes, square passes, oblong and octagonal passes. We get 'staff' passes (but they still aren't enough to allow us to watch Depeche Mode from the stage). There's catering enough to feed a reasonably sized third-world country, can-go areas, no-go areas, can-go that become no-go suddenly, crew of all shapes and sizes of baseball cap, buses and trucks and drivers and (separate band-members') limos, caravans and huts and games machines and a swimming pool, ironing boards and ladies with sewing kits. Music as big business? It's confirmed when I see a filing cabinet being wheeled up the ramp onto the stage.

We crack champagne and soak sun – several Scottish skin-types soon resemble the salmon served up for dinner. Showtime! Here we go boys (and girls), over the top we go again, into the unknown. The crowd are appreciative, they know 'Rocks', 'Come Together', 'Loaded', etc., but seem to be saving themselves for 'the Mode'. It's been a long while since the Scream have played to an 'impress-me' crowd and these mothers are gonna need some shaking up, that's for sure. The biggest gripe, of course, is that in forty-five minutes, just when everything's well-oiled and firing, you're cut in your prime, no chance for completing the job. Rock 'n' roll does not have a timetable!

A plane flies overhead lit with the flashing message 'Welcome Primal Scream' and here come the US record company reps (on wheels) and it's all getting a bit *Spinal Tap* – 'Hi, I'm [Artie Fufkin] head of marketing and exploitation. Loved the album, just a-dor-ed the show.' 'Well, hi guys, I'm [Artie Fufkin] associate deputy secretary of …??

Hey, I'm a fan, you know what I'm saying.' Etcetera. Etcetera.

We drive back to Frisco and check into the Phoenix, probably the funkiest hotel in the whole US of A , owned and run by gays, as liberal as you like, with wild art, sculpture and kitsch all over the place, a pool after Warhol and flanked by Miss Pearl's Jam House, which serves the greatest Jamaican food and killer daiquiris. Hotel policy: live and let live. We will.

FRI 13 MAY – DAY OFF – SAN FRANCISCO – UP, UP AND AWAY IN A BEAUTIFUL BALLOON

After some sleep, everyone's on a shopping and drinking tip, so it's off to Haight-Ashbury, the birthplace of psychedelia and all things hippy. To this day its a cool place to hang, and now has the odd hip-hop shop and dance-record emporium wedged between the bongshops. Innes is lost in a sea of pink tracksuits and Charley's Angels posters, Throb's pimping it in rose-coloured star shades and Bob's record-hunting (he pulls in a wicked Clash poster). We bump into the crew and the red wine flows. The cry goes up for 'balloons!', and before we know it we're back at the Phoenix falling round the pool, high on nitrous oxide. Grown men laugh helplessly – thank God for Denise, Henry and Steve Sidelnyk, who return from town (equally happy, equally enthused) and instil a bit of decorum into the proceedings. The night ends in the Jam House: oysters in a chilli sauce, tequila chasers, brain-cell coladas; Oz the soundman on a rampage; a twenty-strong hen night getting more drunk than us; two runaways from the north of England; its all getting hazy and it's definitely time to leave. And with an early start tomorrow we'd best get some sleep …

SAT 14 MAY – SHORELINE MOUNTAINVIEW – GIVE US A KITSCH CAMPEONES

Well, Primal Scream have a reputation for not being the most punctual of people and it's always a struggle to get out of a hotel to meet a plane, or a train, or a soundcheck, or a gig, etc. But I'm afraid the cover is blown, boys. It's easy. Just tell everyone that the FA Cup final is on TV. At 5.30 am just a mere tap on the Throb's door, where in the past it's occasionally had to be kicked in (accepted tour expense), and he's up, marching around the pool in Man U shirt and matching Bill Grundies. Innes is wide-o, excited by the draught-Guinness prospect of the Irish bar we're heading for. Tour manager Trigger, up for the cup in CFC away style. Duffy too, wondering if at last he can be allowed to celebrate the Villa's league cup victory over United during the British tour, which almost got him thrown out of the band (well, at least the hotel). The crew are also in attendance, it's 7 am in the Abbey Tavern, San Francisco, the black stuff's flowing as we witness the (slightly undeserved) destruction of Chelsea. Trigger at one point has to be held back from the screen and is later inconsolable as the United posse order doubles for the double. I can barely walk when I leave the place and it's still only 9.30! Breakfast of Absolut and cranberry at the hotel, Throb's nearly sinking in the pool, and so the day proceeds. It's going to be a long one.

For the two-hour drive out to the Shoreline amphitheatre it's a total boozing frenzy in the back lounge: Duffy's dancing Beavis-style, Bob's miming into a champagne bottle, the Seeds and the Chocolate Watch Band are pounding us at volume 11. It's a happy, raucous scene – Denise joins in and rock-chicks it up. As a result, the band hit a better stride at the gig and the smiles are flowing, except from Trigger. Throb and I try consoling him back at Miss Pearl's, with double shots of tequila and margaritas by the score, while Duffy is upstairs destroying Stevie Molloy's room. I see Trigger off to bed, waiting patiently along the way while he offers out the swimming pool, then try to coax Robert to a party where Garth, an English DJ

I know, and the Wicked crew are playing. As Throb slides off the barstool and lies semi-comatose on the floor I know I'm fighting a losing one. It's left to me and Abbot (Creation top bod over for the proceedings) to carry the torch. A full-on night of San Fran techno, a chance meeting with some old East End faces, Nigel Benn's bobbing and weaving in the corner and it's all gone totally surreal by the time we find ourselves at 10 am, full-on sun with no shades, trying to weave our way through the middle of the San Francisco marathon as clowns and tutu-clad runners flash by us, while on the corner a tinny sixties cover band plays 'I Saw Her Standing There'. Some thirty hours that was.

SUN 15 MAY – CONCORD PAVILION, CA – ALL ABOARD THE CRYSTAL SHIP

After crashing in Duffy's room we are soon rudely awoken by him fanning us with a huge palm leaf and talking utter gibberish. You'd have thought it had been him up all night tucking untold narcotics away. He is truly amazing. He's off with Bob and Hartie to the Sunday service at the church of John Coltrane. Much as I want to go, at this stage I can't stand. They later return very excited, having been 'bathed in light' and accusing the rest of us of being the 'unclean'.

Lunchtime remedy of frozen margaritas to revive whilst spectating as the Throb marks off Miss Pearl's cocktail list, necking one of each. Unbelievable. The goal posts are moving …

Anger in Concord as the soundcheck is cut. Trigger has his work cut out restoring calm before the band go onstage. Turns out to be the best of the three gigs so far, a new addition to the show being the chick who hit the stage writhingly, on a beeline for the Throb, wanting to play his guitar, and seemingly, wanting to play him. Her modesty is preserved by the appearance of her worried-looking boyfriend from the front row. He decides to show who's in charge by leaping on and getting off with her centre stage. Only in America.

Post-gig it's the big moment. We've been invited, for the first time, into the Depeche inner sanctum for some meet and greet. Only Martin Gore is there, pleasant and smiling and showing a deft hand at table football. We eat, drink and be merry and whack the 'Jailbird' remixes on the stereo, while scores of awestruck fans hover and ogle. There's one girl, kicking back cool against a wall, wearing a mini-skirt of absolutely no point and pouting. She's fourteen. Then she introduces the other half - her mum! And a right mother and daughter double act that turned out to be. The crystal's kicked in and everything's in double time, Molloy's on a rant and Duffy's in love with the pinball machine. Molloy's rant has now become a rampage as he struggles to get the troops buswards. By now several members of the party are showing advance signs of STP syndrome and in all honesty it gets messier and seedier as the night proceeds. Mother and child reunion.

MON 16 MAY – SLIM'S, SAN FRANCISCO – FEAR AND LOATHING IN SAN FRANCISCO

Looks say it all. They have to – no one's talking. Psychosis overdrive. But the bonus of the day is tonight it's the Scream's own gig. A (semi) secret affair for local radio 105FM at Slim's club down amongst the darker districts of this beautiful city, a chance at last to break some sweat, make some noise and get some fucking rocks off. Throb's got a foxy chick front-row, literally dribbling on his boots – apart from the truck-stop muscles and tattooed chest, she's a stunner. A rousing set that everyone needed badly. To Innes' dismay, Duffy has blown the whistle that it's his birthday and Ren (US) management have laid on a birthday cake and (more)

champagne. Though appreciative, Innes rightly remarks that it's a bit of a waste as none of these fuckers ever eat. Still, everybody's happy and ready for the first overnighter on the bus, through the Nevada desert to the end of civilization as we know it: Las Vegas.

TUES 17 MAY – ALADDIN THEATRE, LAS VEGAS – INTO THE BELLY OF THE BEAST

There's a mass wake-up to check out the amazing landscape that stretches for miles all around us. The driver's in a rush – he don't want to get stuck in the desert, no way – he don't want no bus fry-up, man. And there it appears, surely the maddest, most ridiculous, avaricious place on the planet, and therefore also one of the most intriguing. We stumble into the Aladdin Hotel reception and can't find the check-in desk for the thousands of slot machines, poker tables and roulette decks, populated (even at this 9 am hour) by blue-rinse fortune-seekers and Mr and Mrs ever-hopefuls of mid-west, USA. So cheap to eat, the restaurant looks like it's holding a convention of the obese. It's sheer piggery. There ain't a face big enough to stuff all that food in. As Innes observes, 'a third off every plate of food in America and you could easily feed the rest of the world'. It really does become a bit obscene. Our breakfast is constantly interrupted by badly dressed and oddly shaped girls, screaming 'Keno!', trying to entice us into a bingo-style numbers game played while you eat.

As we are playing the Aladdin Theatre (up there in lights with Dino, Liza and Frankie) there isn't far to go, and in reality there isn't far to go in Vegas anyway. Why walk thirty, twenty or even ten minutes in the soaring heat to find more of the same?

After more liquid than lunch, Throb and Molloy head for the tables, Bob goes for nod, Innes, D and Henry go mooching and for protection I go into myself. A posse arrives in town out of LA. The dressing room is full of people, staring rather than talking - it's a strange atmosphere. The gig is in the first indoor venue of the Mode tour, a mere 7000-seater and again, the Scream do what they need to do but, frustratingly, are unable to do more than that.

We march off into the lights and land on Caesar's Palace where high-haired greco-roman tack nymphs ply us with free drinks at the tables. The Long Island iced teas take their toll and the casino takes our money. Bobby, finding the whole Vegas experience 'soul-less', freaks out and gets out while I, Throb, George Drakoulias and Kev P, a stand-up comedian of some repute from the UK south coast, keep playing the wheel. Throb and I get out on top, but it should be noted that collectively, as a group, the casino still took us. That's the way it works, along with oxygen pumped in to keep the punters awake. By now, a search party is out for our group, the bus is waiting to leave – we are busy investing our winnings in party 'material' for the journey in a skyrise hotel room with the lights and desert stretched out for miles below us. Once we do return, the Clash goes on back-lounge for a mad word-for-word sing-up. The desert and landscape of Arizona does not let us down. *This* is America.

WED 18 MAY – DESERT SKY AMPHITHEATRE, PHOENIX – SAY KIDS, WHAT TOWN IS IT?

At 10 am Duff, Molloy and Throb have plotted up in the open-air hospitality and when we leave at 2 am next morning they still seem to be in the same place. It's Martin's birthday and his close companion for the day is a speaking Beavis & Butthead doll that constantly thrusts at people. The doll's one and only line: 'That sucks!' Molloy is guarding the dressing room with a Flintstone club, instilling a jovial fear backstage. Washing machines get plenty of usage and someone goes out for new socks and grundies.

The boys aren't happy, the drinks rider is three hours late and the come-down's sooner. During the show Bob gazes deep into the children of Phoenix while Denise is working overtime – hail the queen of 'rock 'n' soul'. Bus driver John (boy of the Bible Belt) is getting increasingly touchy and a note is despatched for all to see, listing the cost of repair of any item/area on the bus that gets trashed. A stupid thing to do; several lines already have ticks and people bid for the remainder. This could be a dear old bus ride as a disgruntled squad head for LA.

THURS 19 MAY – DAY OFF, LOS ANGELES – CONTEMPLATING PARANOIA BUT TOO STONED TO THINK ABOUT IT

We're parked off Hollywood Boulevard, someone's left the bus door open, the a/c's frozen over and now broken down and people have started roasting in their bunks. Band in a casket. Not a happy crowd meander the lobby of the famous Roosevelt Hotel – proper sleep is needed, collective chill-out in order, so my proposed band photo shoot is postponed and the limo sent packing. This hotel is supposed to be haunted with spirits of Hollywood's golden age – I wonder, though, what the ghosts may make of the sight of Duffy or Molloy stalking the corridors during the night? Rumour is they've left town already. Duffy's been sprung as the pillow thief: five are found in his pit, which is a mystery as he rarely makes it to his bunk. Faxes start turning up from the European tour – the Golden Tulip Hotel in Amsterdam wants £700 for Throb's guitar tech Jason's little night out (in his room), the Swedish promoter is after £800 for a Gothenburg mirror, a grand for a lift in Berne …

The Hockney-painted pool gets its fair share of use (quicker than washing?), then it's down to hip shopping/bar/hang-out street, Melrose, where, being a day off, everyone proceeds to get totally steaming. Alex Nightingale turns up on the Virgin flight from London, accompanied by gossip, football scores, journalist and old friend Helen Mead, and a couple of bottles of champagne. Throb is now back from Melrose, thrashing about in the lobby, not a happy man – it takes a nation of millions to calm him down.

Basically, he's having the kind of occasional outburst that everyone on tour needs to have once (or twice) in a while. Some take a long time to crack, some are off after a day, but you can bet your bottom dollar that by the end of a long tour (and especially in America) even the calmest of souls will have been reduced to a screaming, irrational maniac, completely immune to reason. Given the closeness of a dozen or more people living in each other's pockets, given the fractured sleep patterns, the heat, the tiredness of huge drives (1000 miles sometimes), the outside influences of booze and whatever else, and the madness that is America itself, it's a wonder anyone returns home sane. No one's complaining of course, but whatever you do in life has its own set of problems and stresses, and this game's no different.

So there's a four-hour void while Robert is calmed and the bar gets a good syphoning. I go off with Bob, Helen and her photographer Sally to Pasadena to take a drink with Paul Weller who is in town for the final show of a short US jaunt. We sit under the stars discussing music (of course), South Africa, Chelsea's Wembley defeat, the Jam's '78 American tour supporting Blue Oyster Cult (!), Vespas, peyote and much, much more while getting mashed on Irish coffees and the occasional blunt. Back at the Roosevelt, I'm attacked by a hysterical Filipino woman who screams I've taken her bag containing a cash delivery she's been waiting three weeks for. Even the film and cameras in my bag doesn't convince her it's mine and she's soon led away by security. Bizarre. We bat on with crew boys Murray, Jacko and Chrissy Ridge. There's weed on the go that I'm convinced has

been soaked in acid and which leaves me wandering/haunting the corridors 'til I find my bed; unable to undress I wake some hours later curled up on the corner of a king-size bed, boots on and using my jacket as a blanket. Sad. I often think what a waste it is to have hotel rooms when the most anyone does is dump their bags, throw some water on face, ending the night on the floor in some other part of the building. One room would do for the boys and another for Denise. What a saving!

FRI 20 MAY – IRVINE MEADOWS, CA – OOH AAH, ESCOBAR

Meet by the pool. Aretha and Marvin the perfect soundtrack for the traffic-laden three-hour crawl to Irvine Meadows. Past trailer parks with little ragged Stars and Stripes flying sadly from caravan tops, rooms with a (freeway) view, sunbathers high on monoxide. Past industrial theme parks, passed by Porsches full of card sharks. Breakfast does the rounds, a bowl of amphetapuffs. Spirits are high, all ready for the big one. The stadium is huge, we do pictures in the sun. The gig's OK, people are dancing, but we start to wonder if they really get it. Can 'Higher than the Sun' really be explained to a Valley Girl? It becomes clear that these Californians are partisan beyond comprehension.

Throb's on a mad one and unidentified objects are flying about in the dressing room, so the fixed-grin brigade hover in and bolt out. Best lines: 'Hey, loved the show last night' (the band hadn't played), 'You guys RRROCK!', and to Denise, a hard one to beat, 'Seriously, babe, its happening for you, but ya gotta dump those bums.'

Our lighting man Andy's bar and grill is open, wedged between two trucks, and where the best moonlight margaritas are served up. The hospitality area becomes a Scream convention, Needsy's Jail remixes kicking the proceedings into gear. A beach boy gets over-lairy and gets the nut stuck on him from one of the Manchester contingent. It's all getting a bit boss-eyed and tension hangs in the air. We should leave. By the time we get back to LA the clubs are closed so a mass debate regarding the state of the Bolivian economy is held in one of the hotel rooms. Ghosts? It's time to leave when I realize I'm having a conversation with one of them.

SAT 21 MAY – BLOCKBUSTER, SAN BERNADINO – THE DAY OF THE DUFF

Boy, ain't no one can compete with this bloke today, I'm sure he's on delayed reaction and still thinks it's his birthday. He's been up all night and, after insulting Helen and Sally to the point that they won't board the bus, it's suddenly Duff against the world sparked off by a disputed (breakfast) bar bill. To Molloy and Nightingale, 'I'm not listening to you Freddie Starr, or your mate. I love you Alex, but at the moment I FUCKIN' HATE YOU!' Then, 'I'm looking at an exit sign Alex, and it's glowing …'. The lone member of big fat Ron's claret and blue army is absolutely raging.

Close to the arena there's a 'Renaissance' fair, where the middle-class white kids dress up and fake roughing it in 'Olde England' then return to suburbia in $20,000 camper vans.

Duffy, in a mock 'inn', 'Doth thou have a goblet of Guinness?'
Barman, 'You got ID?'
Duffy, 'They never said that in the fourteenth century!'

Back at the gig, the Primals' performance is affected with an edge most in the crowd can't relate to. Safe Californian homes.

We tail the Duff as he goes wild amongst the front rows, screaming

'Personal Jesus' at the top of his voice during Mode's set. He's running rings around the over-hyped security, miming scissor punches and badly upsetting the steroid college jocks who cry that he is obstructing their view. From here it's all downhill, and uphill, and downhill as we chase the hare Duff all over the stadium.

Post-gig during the Scream v. Mode table-football match we struggle to keep the Duff off the pitch. He is on the most hysterical top form and making more noise than the 15,000 crowd who've slipped away politely into the night. He enters into a happy shouting match with Martin Gore, both seeing who can scream 'Shaft' the loudest, for some bizarre reason. Arriving back at the hotel, we find him in his bunk, refusing to leave the bus and singing 'Who are ya' repeatedly from behind the curtain. The reception won't give Steve Molloy the Duff's key and asks, 'Well, where is Mr Duffy?', at which point Steve carries the comatose Duff into the lobby, dumps him on the desk with, '*Here* is Mr Duffy.' He is duly handed the key and Duff is dispatched finally to bed. But can you keep him down? No way – about three hours later he appears at Throb's window trying to step through the sliding door. Nutcase.

SUN 22 MAY – WHISKY, LOS ANGELES – HOLLYWOOD HIGHS

I go with Hartie to set up a photo shoot and Bob, Andrew, Robert, Denise and the Duff (in some nick he is), join us later. The gig tonight is a Hell's Angels' benefit for a member that is about to receive the outrageous sentence of life that now in the States is automatic after a person has committed (any) three felonies. They could be three medium offences but three strikes and you're out, boy. (Paul Weller had been most unimpressed about this gig a couple of nights earlier. 'Yeah, what's that, then? What's he, a murderer is he, what did he do? Bite some kid's head off did he? Eh? Eh?' Once a mod …)

After the soundcheck and a chat with Steve, the felon in question, people split – I go with Andrew, Denise and our LA man on the ground Las Borsai to the Ren management barbecue high in the Hollywood hills where it's a bit too full-on and tinselly, Californian loud and rammed out. Depeche are in attendance, along with other such luminaries, we stay long enough for a bottle of 'poo then cut down to Barney's to have some tuck-in and get slammed on those good old Long Island iced teas. Our crew are in full quota across the room, suitably 'relaxed' and in happy mood. Hence the gig is great, back to the groove, it's time for a full set, time for a full sweat. Mass pogoing breaks out, led by a Brighton away crew and it's a stormer. The rhythm section's mustard, the guitars are firing, Duff's playing far beyond his hangover and Bob and D dance the night away. With barely enough time for a line for the ladies it's across the Sunset Strip to the Viper Room (scene of River Phoenix's demise) and the band are drunkenly pushed onstage (not before Bob G is rushed out the side door to paint the Sunset pavement with his stomach) by George Drakoulias and whack out a bonus set on borrowed gear to the assembled lucky few. 'Rocks' and 'Jailbird' in a punk-rock stylee! Literally rounded up on the street by a rampant Molloy who's desperate to avoid a mass exodus into deepest, darkest Hollywood. The bus is leaving soon. At 4 am I see them off on a 700-mile journey to Salt Lake City, a place of no-go for me due to japes in younger years. Take it easy, boys, the county jail is not a nice place. Keep it going, keep it together and do your damnedest to educate, agitate, (dis)organize!

Two weeks was more than enough on this abominable tour. There'd always be something to have a laugh about with the likes of Duff and the Throb but it'd be a sorry state of affairs if you ended up constantly touring like that. A load of old cack. Might be where the

money is, but then again, there's a load of money in a bank and you wouldn't want to work there, would you?

Most of the summer is spent in London, but to tell you the truth I'm not having a good time. Don't know what it is but I keep feeling bad. Psychologically bad, physically bad, fucking awful without explanation. Admittedly, the personal stuff from last year I haven't quite put to bed, but it's more than that. My head's in bits. It really comes on top at a Rock Against Racism rally in Brockwell Park when I find myself panicking about nothing at all. Running out the park, hiding in the back of my car, fearing people. I've never feared anything in my life, but now I've got the fear and I've got it bad. It should have been obvious but before long it dawns: the tally man's been, left a note to say he'll be back. And I owe big time. As the saying goes, you don't get nothing for nothing. Now is the time, the price to pay. I hold my hands up. It's all my own work, no one forced me and I don't want sympathy. I can only count myself lucky it wasn't worse – some don't come back. There's a pattern of sorts that begins to emerge. You can trace it back to that Christmas batch of pure MDMA. Seems everyone who touched it is now a bit touched and some are in a seriously terrible state. I'm not suggesting for a moment that any of the other gear has been actually good for me, but this was the proverbial amber light.

I'm now very touchy about getting too involved with anything that might send me spinning and I keep my profile very low. I have to come out of retirement for Reading, though. The Scream are headlining the festival and I couldn't miss that. Especially as Mick they're-dancin'-not-fightin' Jones has been invited as an encore guest for a rousing 'Jail Guitar Doors'. Most of the pictures I took of this event are unfortunately blurred. Well, you try pogoing with a camera. I'm not so sure Depeche Mode's Dave Gahan's been invited, because what he's playing on the harmonica has got nothing to do with what anyone else onstage is doing. What a bleedin' racket. All the money you've got, boy, buy yourself some lessons.

A couple of days later we're in Madrid for a gig in the bull-ring with the Red Hot Chilli Peppers who, I have to say, don't disguise the fact that they fancy themselves a bit. In a dispute backstage they make the mistake of trying to run our 'end'. Bad move that. FATTY! DON'T! Put him down!

Through Brian Eno's valiant efforts to raise awareness and cash for the charity War Child by selling works of art by musicians, I end up representing Primal Scream and donating some pics. Quite an honour to be amongst such distinguished company as Bowie, the Ig, McCartney, etc. The gallery launch at Flowers East in Hackney is a star-studded affair and the paparazzi are out in force. You can't move for limos, and fans of the mighty throng the streets. As I pull up on my '63 Lambretta there's a rush of photographers who crowd round flashing. 'It's Pete Townshend, I'm telling you!' I take my helmet off and they're gone. Hang on! I used to be in the Kidz Next Door, I'll have you know. Wankers. Couldn't take a good picture if they tried. Leeches. Despicable occupation.

Thailand's most famous traffic cop, who last year caused havoc when he switched all the traffic lights to green at a busy crossroads and danced in the road, is back – and denying that he ever had any problems.

That's just a clipping I found in my diary. He sounds like a right card, unlike the shitcunt who cracked my ribs on the Criminal Justice Bill march. I swear to God, take your uniform off and let's have it one to one without your mates. You think I really want to be a test dummy for your brand new long-handled baton? Now it's obvious in our society that the ability to police ourselves has long since gone, so to be a fan of All Coppers Are Bastards is just naive. The more we distance ourselves from them, the more the seige mentality sets in. I also think there are plenty of coppers, which I'll also agree are a shrinking minority, that start in the force with the best intentions: serving the community, protecting the people, even the bloke on the march with two goats on a string.

But that's no excuse whatsoever for the no-number bully boys that love to crack heads. So I was taking pictures. And it was a carnival, and happy, until you bastards started. And when you go wading in, what do you expect people to do? Of course they'll fight back.

I went down in Park Lane, gasping for air, thought the bastard had punctured my lung. They left me there for half an hour. Next time I'm on a demo and you go down, do I turn to people and say ease off, or do I put one in myself? Think about it, you divvy plod cunt.

In a separate incident the same night in London west, Bobby and friends had reconvened after the Heavenly Social at the house of the Nightingale Al. After a neighbour's complaint about the volume control, it's a trifle heavy-handed when a hurry-up shows, packed to the hilt with overtime smiles. I suppose Alex didn't help himself when the lead copper said that the music was too loud. Loud? LOUD? I'LL SHOW YOU LOUD. As he turns the volume up to 11 and breaks out in a pogo. Course they nicked him. Lucky they didn't commit him. But in the melée they've got Bobby Gillespie pinned to the wall, likewise some girlfriends, who make an attempt to come to his aid. London's burning.

The songwriters decamp to Ibiza in order to write songs. It's just the Throb, Bob, Innes and Murray the muzz holding the fort. I skip out there for a short one, even though breathing is still difficult. We go exploring on bikes and get a bit lost. We make it back to the tarmac road and we're one man short. Stay here, Throb, and I'll go back and look. We'd cut on a mountain dirt-track in search of the bay. I see the scooter wrapped in the trees. Oh fuck, Willie Wallace is over the edge. Call the coastguards, man the boats. Cancel that. This bloke's got one on Jesus. Crown – that's nothing, this one has got a headful of thorns. Staggering along, picking them out one by one. I try not to laugh. I haven't got a chance. I conserve my energy not to wet myself. What happened, Andrew? 'Aye, well I was coming round the bend and a four-wheel nearly took me out. I ended up in the ditch but they helped me out. Four giggling superbabes dressed in string. Out o' order, man, out o' order …'

From here to Colombia, onto Peru, cross into Bolivia, down to Chile. Annie Nightingale's the one who's got me buzzed, and I'll thank her for ever for putting me on, for there's nothing more mind-blowing than a solar eclipse. Who needs narcos when there's that kind of gear about?

I take a side trip to see a Colombian boy I've sponsored over the years, a couple of hours outside Cali (not so much a child any more, and a wizard on the pitch. He'll emulate local hero Asprilla, I'll bet a penny a peso). It's double mind-blowing. Sponsoring him cost £3 a week, and what's that back home, not even a couple of beers. That alone is easy, no more to be said. But having been to the village and seen where that three quid goes, believe me it's worth its weight in gold. Get on it. Sponsor a child today. Plan International. The number's in the phone book.

Sadly, there's a downside to this particular trip. Dialogue breaks down between me and the Jen and there's a realization that it's all gone totally and irretrievably Peter Tong. Things have been difficult

since I went up the wall, but this distance has seemed to cement the rift. It's something I don't want, but I'd better accept quickly, before it does my head in again. Déjà vu, I hate you. So what do I do, against all reasonable advice. Cancel my ticket, remain in Bogotá and get on the kind of bender that changes your name. It actually did me the world of good. Colombian girls, Colombian rum. Colombian. You could do a lot worse.

So by the time I come home I'm ready to face up, and race up to Stoke and catch up with the Scream. No end to the bend.

This is the second UK tour of the year, populated by all the usual suspects, complemented by support band Sabres of Paradise and DJs the Dust Brothers. These brothers sank without trace, not long after a dispute over names with the US version. Renamed themselves the Chemical Brothers – it'll never catch on. And that Sabres lot – bang out of order. The whole lot of 'em, trying to sit down to breakfast with their pants on their head in Norwich, of all places. They'll end up giving the rest of us a bad name.

Look, this tour is every bit as good as the first. I could weave a tale that would come in volumes, not books, but at the end of the day, month or year it's best summed up in a few simple facts:
Primal Scream are so on-form it's silly.
The vibe on this tour is the best ever.
I am having the time of my life.
Don't know where it will end but I hope it never does.

But I can't leave London out. In a break with tradition there are two shows at the Empire, Shepherd's Bush, then all back to normal for the end of tour at Brixton Academy. Mental by anyone's standards. Paul Weller turns up – well up for the crack. 'So Sad About Us' in a duet with Bob, and every mod in the house sheds a tear. Noel Gallagher on solo guitar, and you've got your money's worth.

Meanwhile back at the hotel …
'Mr Fowler.'
'Yeah, what?'
'Your ironing is done. '
'What?'
'If you'd like to come down to reception …'
Phone slammed down. 4 am. And repeated through the night. That's Robbie Fowler of Liverpool, in town for tomorrow's match against QPR. And that's the Archbishop on his case. As a result I think they only got a point.

Last night, Bob's room, and there's no sitting around. The Small Faces are on the stereo, as loud as ever. A paranoia-free zone. Dance and dance until you fall off the bed.
'Excuse me, sir, you're way beyond check-out time.'
It's 5 pm and there's only me and Anna Haigh (superstar singer from Bocca Juniors and star of the classic Wiz film of Flowered Up's 'Weekender') left in the room: there were a dozen the last time I looked.
'Sir! I'm going to have to ask you to leave.'
'All right! I'm going, I'm going, just let me sort out my bags. Oi, where are my bags, what have you done with my bags? My *cameras!*'
'Calm down, sir, this isn't your room.'
'Oh yeah.'

Back in that office-cum-apartment, barely five miles away. Silence as opposed to pandemonium; loneliness as opposed to a stream of candidates up for a lark.

Comedown.

Above Balloon enthusiast. San Francisco.
Below Big Jet Plane. Fly me home to the promised land.

Above Trig. Muzz. Jacko. Molloy. Innes. Jase. Throb. Duff. The streets of San Francisco. 7a.m. Cup Final Day.
Below Two-nil at Wembley. I wonder who to?

MTV New York.

Denise Johnson. Concord Pavilion. California

Left Nappy dug-out. Hartie's tribute to Funkadelic. Copthorne Hotel. London.
Above 'Who are ya! Who are Ya!' California. **Below** Sister D and Brother Muzz.

Above George Clinton and Bobby G. Backstage. Brixton Academy. London.
Below 5a.m. I staggered out of the lift on the 16th floor and … Duffy and Alex. Sheraton Hotel. Brussels.

Bob G. Britannia Hotel. Manchester.

The Throb. Old Trafford. Manchester.

Above San Francisco.
Below Best (and only) meal of the day. Amphetapuffs. Leeds.

Cardiff.

'Jail' video. Luton.

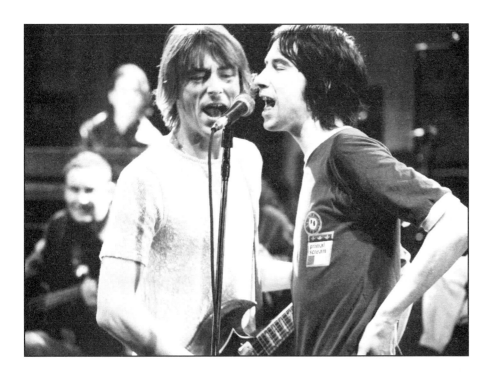

Above Bob and the Modfather. Shepherds Bush Empire. London.
Below George and the Scream. MTV Studios. New York.

Above Steve Sidelnyk. Dublin.
Left and **Below** Sant Josep. Ibiza.

Above Irvine Meadows. California. **Right** Duff and one of his many mates. Roosevelt Hotel. Hollywood.
Below Innes and Mick Jones. I'm watching you. Unlike half an hour earlier when Mick had swung round on stage taking Andrew's hat clean off. A classic rock 'n' roll moment. Reading Festival.

Anyone seen Throb? 'Jail' video. Luton.

Needsy. We're well into the tour by this point. Cambridge.

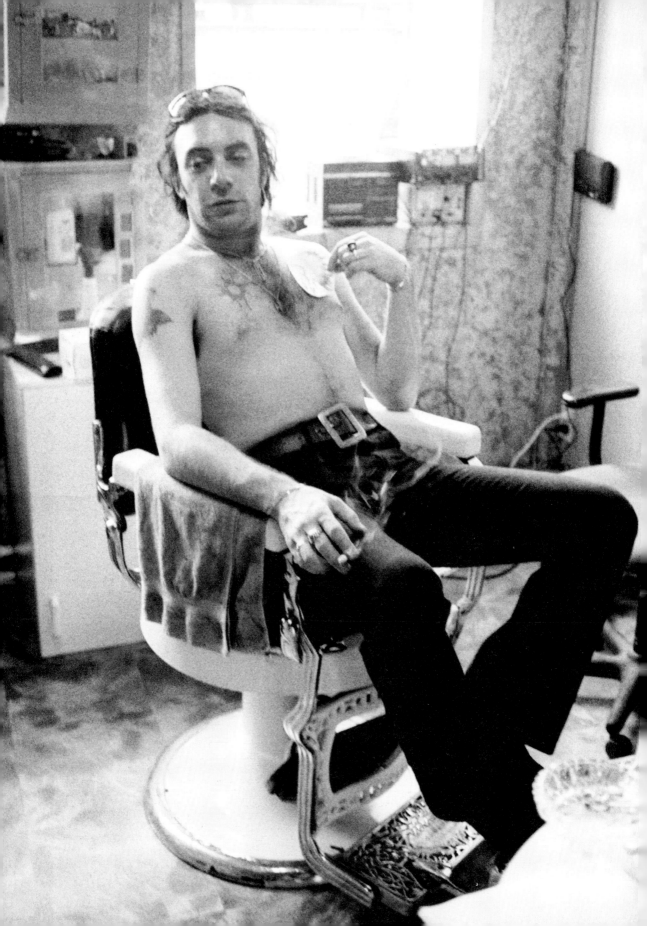

1995

Sadly, we come to the last leg of the 'Give Out' tour which begins with an antipodean adventure as the Scream are booked on the roving 'Big Day Out' festival. Nine gigs in eight cities in twenty days in the middle of the summer down under. That would put a smile on anyone's face; it certainly puts one on mine. My flight to Auckland has a stopover in LA. Some stopover – it's a wonder I didn't end up on the news. My friend Jess is a pal of Kate Moss and, coincidentally, will be in the States at the same time, helping to throw a surprise twenty-first for the girl who's probably the most famous thing to come out of Croydon – apart from the Damned of course. How that leads to me fighting with papparazzi alongside prime time pop stars and supermodels outside the Viper Room, as an Aussie soap star is rushed out on a stretcher, is anyone's guess, but you can't come all this way and have a quiet night in, can you?

The Scream are coming in on Air New Zealand and I've tried to book myself a seat. Their plane is full, but the one I get booked on departs at almost the same time and, oddly enough, from the very next gate. They have just flown eleven hours from London and can't you tell. Sodden drunk. The US authorities won't let us convene, so we're kept apart by a huge glass wall. We mock touching hands like lovers through the divide, though Duffy's one better, pressing his lips for a kiss on the glass which is just as well, as he looks like he needs the help in standing up. Fatty is charging about, screaming and hollering, and the smokers are in full revolt. Apparently, LAX is a total no-smoking zone, which is fair enough, but that doesn't stop the boys being sold packs of 200 from the duty-free shop. It's hypocrisy in full effect and I'd be pissed off as well.

We say our goodbyes until Auckland and I'm now alone with a fun pack I'd brought along for the troops. It's a mental flight and I don't sleep a wink, wandering during Hawaii and Fiji stopovers like a man possessed. When I finally arrive in Auckland two days later (lost one on the date-line and I want it back) I approach customs and am asked for 'anything to declare'. I open my mouth and a filling falls out. I'm as bewildered as they are, but shake my head no and pocket the offending article.

'What's your business here?'
'Well, I've come to do pictures for a band on the Big Day Out …'
'What band?'
'Primal Scre–'
'Come this way, sir.'

There then followed a two-hour interrogation and a full-body search. Ooh, you are awful. Turns out back in LA just after I left, the police turned up and led half a dozen of our tour party away, after Air New Zealand refused to take them any further. Unbeknown to me the stories have broken in NZ of smashed-up planes, drink and drugs. No charges were brought except the ones for six new tickets to Auckland, but it's got the authorities on full alert. Well I've got nothing, at least not any more, and after suffering rants about how E

had changed football and other such tirades that go over their heads, I think they're pleased to see the back of me.

You travel all that way, practically as far as you can go, and when you leave the airport what do you find? Neatly trimmed hedges and garden gates, little pretty pink cottages and field after field of grazing sheep. Rural England back in the fifties. I feel like I came in on the tardis. Thankfully, Auckland's got little to do with that olde worlde charm as a night in the Squid Bar soon reveals. Plenty of cool clothes shops and record emporia, and after a couple of days I'm fast running out of PDs (per diems – daily expenses). Throb and Steve Molloy celebrate their US release by having tattoos while Bob, Hartie and I check for a Bob Marley exhibit. In the running order, the Scream follow Hole and a couple of us have already met the singer in a lift. We said hello and she flopped out her lils. Strange behaviour, but there you go.

Fatty's invested his PDs in a stuffed ram's head and carries it around like a long-lost friend. He's held up at customs as they check out the stuffing and by the time he boards the flight to Melbourne he's practically wearing it on his head.

Our internal air tickets have been organized alphabetically which means my travelling companion is one Martin Duff, who is mad enough at the best of times but on this tour he's reading far too much about aliens and abductions. I think they've already got him. There are times when I'm off it and it's torture, him ranting the whole flight through, and others when he's so funny I'm pissing my pants. He reads newspapers from cover to cover, which is no great feat, except the newspaper is upside-down, and shouts out at the top of his voice during the safety routine.

Under your seat you will find a life jacket.
'LIAR!'
In the event that you should need oxygen, a mask will pop out …
'HOW DO YOU KNOW?'
…take out the whistle …
'WHAT YOU GONNA DO WITH THAT, THEN?'
… and shortly we shall begin our trolley service …
'STOP FUCKING SLACKING AND GET A MOVE ON, THEN!
And so on, and so on.

In Melbourne, the Australian record company are eager to impress and ferries the whole tour party out for a meal. But the first-choice restaurant can't accommodate us and we go from one place to another trying to find food. It's becoming tiresome, so we end up somehow back at the hotel where there's one of those fun-theme gaffs directly next door. It's getting late and there are few options left so we find ourselves among the streamers and balloons as Elvis and Marilyn wait the tables next door. Bob is sat there, obviously with the hump. Our 'waiter' appears and he's a happy, zany 'doc' – 'I have got the remedies for you folk.' I try to tell him we don't need the routine but fail in my interception as he takes his bouncy, plastic hammer that makes a 'funny' squeaky noise, pulls a ridiculous face and turns and whacks Bobby over the head.

'FATTY! FUCKING KILL HIM!'

Luckily for 'doc' word has passed that upstairs in the hotel another kind of doctor is doing the rounds and our table clears before you can say, well – speed!

The tour is a stormer and the vibe unreal. There's just something about Australia that makes you smile, apart from the space cakes. They make your stomach ache, you laugh so much. I don't know if it's the weather or the wide open spaces, but everyone seems so chilled out and each time I come here I immediately feel good, artificial stimulants aside. This is also the most well-organized tour I've ever been on. Not in a sterile, officious US way but the attitude seems to be keep everybody happy – punters, artists, crews alike. Credit due to promoters Lees and West, and all involved in this party on wheels.

On after the Scream are a reformed Cult, Ian Astbury and Billy Duffy, teetotal and straight and all the better for it, I'd say. I'd met them probably ten years before, all attitude, egos and acting like arse. It's a pleasant surprise to find that's long gone and live I reckon they're better than ever. 'She Sells Sanctuary' is total genius, and you'll find us rocking it on the side of the stage. Soon as they're off a mad dash ensues, to find the dance arena in time for Fun-da-Mental who night after night kick it right off. Phenomenal big fat funky beats and a lyrical content to match. Rebel music.

After the Melbourne gig we end up in a fetish club, not so hard core, more fashion and hip. Somebody gifts me a little local pill, and it's instant ascension on the dancefloor to heaven. At least it's the kind of heaven I wanna go to, where the music is pumping and angels in plastic go down on each other directly in front of where I'm dancing. Totally out of order.

In Sydney Kylie and Jason turn up backstage for a chat, though Jason gets caned for his ten-gallon hat ('where d'ya leave your horse, cowboy?' and all that jazz) and a baffled Kylie has to be rescued from Duffy who's explaining in fine detail the lyrics to one of the current big hits: 'See, I've got a friend, right, I've got a friend, I've got a friend, right, called Cotton-eyed Joe, right, and he's been married right, A FUCKING LONG TIME AGO!' Pinned to the wall the poor girl was. Mind you Jason was looking better than the last time I'd seen him.

Everything is going along too well. Haven't had such a good laugh since back at school. Everyone agrees, it's the kind of time when you're with all your pals and you haven't got a care in the world. Times like this seem to get rarer as you get older (I won't say grow up), but this is one of those special times, a once-in-a-lifetime tour. But the wheel was bound to come off somewhere down the line and who should be right there, bang in the middle? Yep.

There's a separate Scream club gig in Brisbane but the atmosphere's tense. People have been overdoing it, staying up late. There's a rift in the band, people missing, others drunk. Up 'til now the band have been playing at the top of their form and when they are on it, it's a case of 'follow that'. But tonight it all falls apart. I've seen better support bands at the Dog and Duck. Regardless of this, amazingly the die-hards in the house show their support and call for an encore. The band are all over the place, rowing backstage, and a couple of us step in and try to shore it up. Innes for some reason drops me a flippant comment, but it's a comment that really hits the spot. What's such a shock is that Andrew is normally as sweet as a nut, we

get on well, and attitude's not his game. I'm badly wound up and it's done me in, to the point that I want to get the first plane out. Not before a bottle of Stoli, and then it's all going up in the air.

We're kept apart for the journey back down the Gold Coast, Denise the comforter as I rant on and on, and an hour later I've calmed down a lot. As we enter the hotel enter Duff stage right. Now he's ranting, and I'd say it's two bottles of Stoli, following me around, and pulling my arm. 'You're like fucking Eric Cantona you are. You're being a prima donna like Eric FUCKING CANTONA!' (News had just reached us of an incident at Selhurst Park.)

'All right Duff, leave it, mate, I just wanna go to bed.'

'I love you, Grant, and I fucking care about you, but you think you're fucking CANTONA, you do!'

'All right, Duff!'

'You're a fucking prima donna like Eric …'

'NNNNNNNOOOOOOOOO!'

The nearest object arcs its way across the lobby. It's a chair. We watch in silence as it glides slo-mo through the air, time suspended, graceful as a … Straight through a marble table. The centrepiece of the whole damn place.

'Quick Duff, run!'

The lift closes just as the hotel's body-builder security types launch themselves at the door and we're barely one floor up when he's off again: 'See what I mean, you're a fucking prima donna you are, you're like ERIC FUCKING CANTONA!'

I wish I'd thrown him instead. This continues in my room as I'm packing my bags and the pair of us drink the mini-bar dry. It's true, he is genuinely concerned, it's just the way he tells 'em. Various tour managers and band members turn up and finally convince me there's no plane tonight and Hartie eventually talks me to sleep.

When morning comes I'm calm but still determined to go, then Bob and Throb take me aside and make me see sense. What remains of the table is now roped off and Trigger is summoned to face the boss. He covers my arse and valiantly attempts to deny our involvement but is stopped in his tracks when the manager produces the video. All on film. Bang to rights. And guess what? It's a Japanese-owned hotel and they want top dollar. So, as it was in the beginning, so shall it be in the end. Trig does some negotiating and secures a good deal, which, unfortunately, does not include the tape. I see Innes at the gig and he holds out his hand. Kiss and make up. Long forgotten. Go on then, I'll have a Guinness with ya.

This is all just as well because I wouldn't have wanted to miss the boat trip for anything in the world. We're staying at a resort called Surfer's Paradise, on the Gold coast by the Tasman Sea. But we leave the high-rises and candy floss behind and take a boat the other way to explore the vast network of inland waterways. Sun and champagne, we've turned into a Duran Duran video. No, we haven't – there aren't any chicks. Lads' day out then, that'll do. A couple of the Cult come along but they don't do too well. After a couple of hours James has passed out while Craig is stark bollock naked and is caught on the bridge trying to steer the boat with his cock. I don't know. The police pay a visit to have a nose around but next thing they've got Fatty boarding their boat, chewing their ears off and soon they're off.

We go for rides in a speed boat (personally, I think our boat has got plenty enough speed) and wind the owner up so much with cries of 'faster' that he nearly wraps the thing and all who sail in it. Close, very close.

Duffy prefers to keep out of the sun, but as every one slaps on sun cream he won't be outdone. He's sat there rubbing cheese and jalapeno dip into his cheeks. Sunning and swimming and dancing and drinking, everyone happy and on raging top form, this was no doubt the big day out, up there in the memory box as a class-A day and made all the better when you know that it's snowing back home. We're lucky people. Very lucky people.

There's an incident in a bar where Throb, Jason and Murray are completely mashed. Some heavies take offence and are seen to be having words. I'm plotted up just across the bar and it doesn't seem to be that out of hand. All of a sudden T and J are up, and in a flash have disappeared. 'Have they gone? They didn't say goodbye,' my friend comments. They'll be back, look they've got two full glasses, there's no way those two would leave drinks behind. But they didn't return and there's got to be a very good reason. Being advised to take a hike, they'd needed no further convincing when a gun had been pushed politely into their ribs.

There are nigh-on tears in Perth when we have to say goodbye, pack up the daiquiris and bury the shorts. On to the final leg of a year-long tour. Japan. Noooo!!! Alex, what's the matter with Brazil? It's a sullen crowd stood waiting for the bus outside Osaka airport later that night. No one is uttering a word. It's difficult when you're wrapped in scarves, hats, hoods and blankets. It's just as well, though, because if it had been the other way round and we'd finished in Australia I doubt that some of us would be back yet.

After a couple of days it's business as usual. What the iceman giveth, the iceman taketh away. The kind of psychosis you have nightmares about. Check for snipers on the roof. I'm not going out - anything on the TV tonight? There's a movie on cable, *Vanishing Point*. About right.

Considering this band have been out for a year, and taking into account that some have also been up for a year there are very few signs of them starting to flag. Going from strength to strength more like, and with the audiences in Japan as up for it as ever, it's a fitting place to end the world tour.

It's also fitting that it should end here for me, in the very same place that it all began. It's not as if it's goodbye or anything like that 'cos I'll always be there and up for a lark, but in terms of pictures I've got plenty enough and it's time to try and make sense of it all. The presentation of the farewell commemorative hotel damages bill has been done and as we've got that out of the way we'd better make it a night of it.

There could be no better way. Getting onstage and doing a couple of songs. It's become a bit of a ritual at the end of a tour. Jacko has a sing, Hartie's got the harmonica. Taking pictures you're so, so close, that sometimes it's frustrating as hell. I hadn't been onstage for a good nine years. Rusty I may be, but Henry runs me through and lends me a bass. 'Jail Guitar Doors' and a version of 'Rocks'. I am flying. No narcotic exists to match this buzz – fucking amazing. From here on in I'm walking on air.

Thanks boys and girls for a truly wicked time. We've had our moments, but families do. Thanks for the music. Keep the faith. Respect is due.

Love Jackson.

Bob G. Throb. Muzzer. Innes. Fatty. Hartie. Jason. D. Sidelnyk. Oz. H. Chrissey Ridge. Gerard. Andy Liddle. Jacko. Duffoir. Trigger. Steve Taylor. Happy, happy days ... Melbourne. Australia.

Above 'Ere Throb, d'ya remember when I went to get Innes that morning when we were all ready to leave and I found him sitting in a room full of bubbles?' Brisbane.
Below Leopalace Hotel. Nagoya. Japan. **Right** Denki Hall. Fukuoka.

Above And all who sail in her. Gold Coast. Australia.
Below Perth.

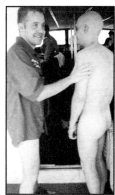

Above 'Get Fatty!' **Right** Oh dear. Gold Coast. Australia.
Below Go on. Sling your hook.

Above Throb and D. The Metro. Melbourne.
Below Innes's Red Cross parcel has just arrived. Liquid Room. Tokyo.

Narita Airport. Tokyo.

Above Always the same old faces, there at the end. Fatty minds the 'Throb, whilst Muzz covers himself up for a good day's sleep. Coogee Beach. Australia.
Below 'So, Bobby G, would you say it was days, or weeks since you've been to bed?' Triple M Radio Station. Brisbane.

Above Tattoo parlour. Auckland. New Zealand.
Below Henry and D. Fukuoka. Japan.

epilogue

The boat trip, twenty years on from the infamous Sex Pistols' 'Jubilee' voyage down the Thames, and what better way to pay homage. The Scream play their first live gig in over two years, there's a new album, *Vanishing Point,* new members, new Scream. Get on board.

As it's a Heavenly special, it's no surprise to find plenty of the same old faces making up the passenger list, some whom are pulling funny ones already. They waste no time, this lot. Fatty's assumed the position usually occupied by the ship's purser, welcoming latecomers with a 'Where the fuck have you been?' No starched collars for him, he's shirtless and sporting the latest in neck-to-waist tattoos. If he thrashes about any more he's gonna tip the boat over. I'm checking for lifebelts.

We've got Mani, ex of the Roses, now blond and by the looks of things having more fun, doing his level best to boot his recent warning of 'it's a young man's game, Granty' right into touch. We haven't even left the quay yet, fella, calm yourself down.

Paul Mulreany, sticksman from the Far East, all the way from Romford. We'll be able to reminisce as we bob on down to the Woolwich Ferry. Used to play on that ferry day in, day out as a kid. Trying to race it back through the foot tunnel. No wonder I get dizzy spells.

The elusive Innes has come up for air after two years in the studio, which would send most of us potty as a jug, but in his case seems to have straightened him right out. There are rumours the band were even turning up by mid-afternoon for sessions as well, ready, willing and more than able. Once or twice even at midday … they do it all the other way round, this lot. The end result is the most drug-fucked, twisted, big-time mash-up of sound since … *Screamadelica*? *Vanishing Point* is totally off its head – mustard. As Fatty keeps shouting at the top of his voice as they play a mini-gig on the tiny patch of floorboard in front of the captain's cabin, 'WELCOME BACK!' I second that. Oh, Fatty already has.

Bob the mod and the Throb giving it to the tourists gawking above on Tower Bridge. Duffy's on the mellotron as we glide past St Paul's – what a sight, with the horn section tucked in somewhere, I think under his keys. Wembley Stadium this ain't. The sound, however, is definitely more U-boat than cruise boat. Producers Lynch and Sherwood have played their part. As for the bass, well we're loving it, man, though I'm sure it's doing the marine life no good at all. Like chucking a grenade in the water … FATTY - DON'T!

'Burning Wheel', 'Kowalski', ' Motörhead' and 'Star'. Amongst others. Rock. The. Boat.

'Star' is beautiful. As I've sat putting this book together over the past couple of months it's given me a lift with every radio play. Kept me going and spurred me on. Just beautiful.

I'm happy, very happy. I've moved on from the office and finally found home – my kind of town. Looking back at the past two years there have been some mean times – that's life – but from where I'm standing now the garden is looking lovely jubbly. And there was many a laugh with the Jagz on the march, and Burnssy Aloof cracking his head on the photo-copier, later found wandering without a memory on the West side (that's what you get when you live in an office). Bob G and the Ems, same old faces every time. Ripping it up on the decks, those mad Disgraceland Friday nights. Special. Too good to be true in the Medicine Bar, meet the sun in Sunday. Checking into Fatty's bar and grill, before you know it, it's Monday. Big support from the *Loaded* magazine boys, right behind me since the US tour '94. They've given me plenty to laugh about: sent me out to cover the 'Star' video in Watts, south-central LA. Like we've not been away, new faces, mates in a day. Up to old tricks and the odd new one too. The boys are back in town.

I've also met the girl to fulfil my dreams - a better partner in crime couldn't exist. She's been there at times when most would have thrown in the towel, a positive support through thick and thin. Mandy Baker, you're a superstar, you'd better believe it, baby.

Seven years on and any wiser? Course. You'd be a muppet if you weren't. Every day's a lesson, if you're willing to learn. Ease up on the accelerator just a bit, you see more that way, and there's *always* something more to see.

Primal Scream? Here we go again then … Ready? Let's have it.

Above Watts. South-Central LA. May '97
Below First live gig for over two years. The Heavenly Boat Party. River Thames. London. June.

Paul Mulreany. 'Star' video. Watts. South-Central LA. May '97.

Mani. 'Star'.

KILL
THE
BILL
CRIMINAL JUSTICE
THE TORIES ARE
THE REAL CRIMINALS

SMASH THE
RACISTS

Spitalfields, London E1. June 1997.